KB274121

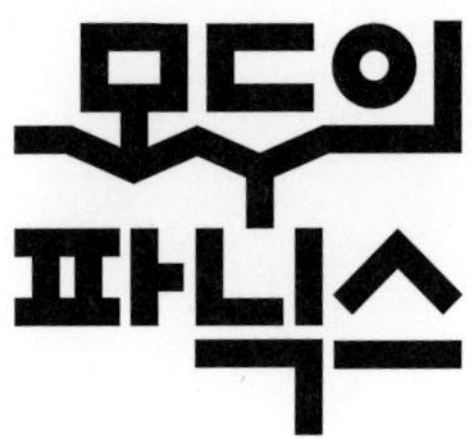

초판 1쇄 인쇄   2026년   2월 10일
초판 1쇄 발행   2026년   2월 26일

발행인   임충배
홍보·마케팅   양경자
편집   김인숙
디자인   서해숙
펴낸 곳   도서출판 삼육오(PUB.365)
제작   (주)피앤엠123

출판신고   2014년 4월 3일
등록번호   제406-2014-000035호

(10882) 경기도 파주시 산남로 183-25
TEL 031-946-3196, FAX 031-946-3171
홈페이지 www.pub365.co.kr

ISBN 979-11-94543-33-6 03730
ⓒ 2026 PUB.365

모의
파닉스

저자의 말

성인을 위한 파닉스 책을 쓰겠다고 생각한 건 아주 오래 전 일이었습니다. 아이들에게 영어를 가르치면서 파닉스 교육의 효과를 톡톡히 봤거든요. 글자가 조합되고 읽히는 원리를 알면 소위 '영어 왕초보' 성인들도 어렵지 않게 영어 단어와 문장을 읽고, 따라서 영어가 조금 더 쉬워지지 않을까 하는 생각에 책을 쓰기 시작했어요. 그게 2017년이었습니다.

책을 쓰는 3년 동안 이 책은 여러 번 모습을 바꾸었습니다. 처음에는 아이들에게 가르치는 것처럼 상세하게 내용을 채우기 시작했어요. 누구나 보면 쉽게 이해할 수 있는 자세하고 친절한 책을 원했어요. 그런데, 막상 쓰고 보니 오히려 내용이 너무 많아 답답해 보이더라고요.

이번에는 조금 '불친절한' 책으로 만들기로 했습니다. 간결하게 최소한의 내용만 담아, 독자 스스로 깨우치기를 바라면서요. 그런데, 파닉스부터 차근차근 영어를 배우려고 책을 집어 든 초급 학습자라면 간략한 내용에 오히려 혼란스러울 수 있겠더군요.

그렇게 거듭된 고민과 여러 번의 수정 끝에 드디어 절충점을 찾았습니다. 이 책은 파닉스를 통해 영어를 시작하려는 분들은 물론 파닉스를 터득해 영어 읽기와 이해에 더 많은 도움을 받고자 하는 분들 모두에게 도움이 될 수 있도록, 설명은 간단히 하되 꼭 필요한 파닉스의 원리를 명확하게 담았습니다.

'파닉스'란 글자와 소리와의 관계입니다. 아마도 거의 모든 분들이 'dog'라는 단어를 읽을 수 있을 거예요. 단어 자체가 눈에 익숙할 테니까요. 하지만 'dog'가 'd-o-g'라는 낱개의 글자들로 이루어졌으며 각 글자의 소리를 부드럽게 연결했을 때 우리가 아는 단어 'dog'의 발음이 된다는 원리를 알면, 비슷한 구조를 가진 'fog', 'frog', 'log', 'blog'등등의 단어들은 물론, 파생되는 단어들까지도 수월하게 읽어낼 수 있습니다. 즉, 각 글자와 그에 상응하는 소리를 배우고 글자들이 모여 단어가 조합되는 패턴을 알아 처음 보는 단어도 읽을 수 있다는 점이 파닉스의 큰 매력입니다.

한 번 제대로 익혀두면 영어 단어와 문장을 읽을 때 두고두고 적용할 수 있는 유용한 '기술(skill)'이 파닉스이며, 이를 통해 기초 읽기 실력도 크게 향상될 수 있습니다. 덤으로 어느 정도 발음 교정도 가능합니다. 영어의 모든 단어가 파닉스 규칙의 적용을 받는 것은 아니지만, 당장 이 책을 한 번만 훑어 보아도 금새 읽어낼 수 있는 단어의 양이 눈에 띄게 늘어날 거예요. 그리고 첫눈에 '소리 내어' '자신 있게' 읽을 수 있는 단어가 늘어갈수록 영어에 대한 어려움과 두려움도 조금씩 줄어들겠지요.

영어 단어를 읽을 때면 왠지 주저하게 되는 분들, 영어를 이제 배우기 시작한 영어 초급자 분들, 영어를 읽고 말할 수는 있는데 내 발음에 확신이 없는 분들. 이 책이 영어에 대해 고민 많은 여러분 모두를 위한 '파닉스 실용서'가 되었으면 하는 바람입니다.

영어를 보는 여러분의 눈, 귀, 입을 활짝 열어 드릴게요. 지금, 저와 함께 시작해요!

추천사

영어를 읽는다는 것은 단어를 보고 소리(sound)도 내고, 그 단어들이 합쳐진 문장과 문단의 의미(meaning)도 안다는 뜻입니다. 궁극적으로는 내용을 이해하는 것이 읽기이지만, 문헌을 구성하고 있는 단어를 소리내지 못하면 의미를 잘 파악하지 못합니다.

예를 들어 세 사람에게 같은 분량의 같은 영어문장을 주고 읽게 한 뒤 시간을 재 각기 1분, 3분, 5분 걸렸다고 칩시다. 세 사람이 모두 처음부터 끝까지 다 읽었어도 1분 만에 읽은 사람이 내용을 제일 잘 압니다. 5분 걸려 읽은 사람은 빨리 읽지 못하는 단어가 많아 이를 읽어야 하는 문제에 매달리느라 미처 의미에 집중할 할 겨를이 없기 때문입니다.

그래서 학자들은 영어 학습자가 일정 시간이 지나도 영어가 향상되지 않으면 학습자의 파닉스를 점검하라고 합니다. 파닉스(phonics)란 글자를 보고 소리를 내는 훈련인데 그렇다고 c는 /k/, a는 /a/, g는 /g/ 하는 식으로 글자와 소리 1:1 연습을 중시하지는 않습니다. 낱 글자 연습보다는 단어를 보고 재빨리 자동적으로 읽기 위한 것이라 공통적인 소리 유형(pattern)을 찾아 단어들을 묶어 연습하게 합니다. 예를 들어 light, fight, sight, night를 잘 읽으면 우연히 plight를 보고 뜻은 몰라도 쉽게 읽습니다. 그러면 문맥 속에서 의미를 유추하는 데 집중할 수 있지요.

니콜의 『모두의 파닉스』는 그런 점에서 참 반가운 책입니다. 시험 위주의 영어공부를 한 중·고생과 성인에게도 파닉스가 필요한데 파닉스는 어린이용 교재 밖에 없는 게 현실이라서요. 단어집과 독해 문제만 푼 사람들은 소리 내어 단어와 문장을 읽지 않고 영어를 학습해 의외로 단어를 유창하게 못 읽습니다. 그러다 보니 계속 노력을 기울여도 영어가 향상되지 않고, 소리 내는 데 자신이 없으니 말하기도 꽤나 힘들어 합니다.

그래서 어린이가 아니어도 파닉스 연습이 꼭 필요한데 이를 잘 인식하지 못하고 있어 안타까운 차, 바로 그 문제를 해결 하는데 도움되는 책이 나왔습니다. 이 책은 pattern을 찾아 단어를 놓고 그 단어로 문장을 만들어 놓았습니다. 큰 소리로 읽다 보면 그야말로 랩을 하는 기분이 들어요. 랩 가사는 각운 혹은 두운을 맞추는 영어 사용자들의 재미있는 말 장난입니다.

어려서부터 구전 동요를 듣고 자라난 원어민들은 랩 같은 음운 맞추기(rhyme)를 무척 즐기는데 영어교육자들은 이를 파닉스 지도에 활용하고 있습니다. 뜻을 몰라도 소리가 재미있어 반복하게 되니 저절로 외워지는데 이는 지도 할 때 효과적이니까요. 그런데 어른은 이미 글자를 숱하게 봐왔기에 외우지 않아도 책의 처음부터 끝까지 큰 소리로 읽어만 봐도 효과가 있습니다.

저자는 13년 간 EBS에서 니콜샘으로 활동하며 영어를 지도한 베테랑입니다. 오랜 세월 학습자들을 보면서 중·고생과 성인들에게도 파닉스가 필요하다는 인식에서 수년 간 공을 들여 단어를 모으고, 문장을 만든 뒤 직접 일러스트까지 했습니다. 작은 책자이지만 일반 파닉스로 교재로는 여러 권짜리 시리즈가 될 양이 담겨 있습니다. 큰 소리로 문장을 읽다 보면 부수적으로 발음도 좋아지고, 나아가 말하기에 자신감도 생깁니다. 입을 열어 소리를 밖으로 내야 하는 연습이기 때문입니다.

이처럼 한 번은 꼭 정리하고 연습해야 하지만 소홀히 하는 것이 파닉스입니다. 교재로 묵독 위주 영어공부를 하신 분들, 그리고 아이의 영어교육에 관심이 커 아이와 함께 동화책을 읽는 부모님들께 특히 이 책으로 연습하시도록 권하고 싶습니다. 이『모두의 파닉스』를 랩처럼 흥얼거리면 읽기가 수월해지는 재미를 흠뻑 느끼시도록 그야말로 모두에게 추천합니다.

언어학 박사 홍 현 주

이렇게
구성했어요

『모두의 파닉스』는 26개 영어 알파벳의 소리로 시작하여, 단모음 위주의 쉬운 단어에서 이중자음·장모음·이중모음 등의 발음 규칙이 포함된 더 복잡한 단어들을 읽을 수 있도록 가이드 합니다. 용어가 어렵게 느껴지나요? 용어는 모르셔도 됩니다. 책 순서대로 패턴을 하나씩 익힌다는 마음으로 도전하세요!

알파벳으로 시작

본격적인 학습에 앞서 Aa부터 Zz까지 글자들의 대표 소리를 알고 있는지 점검해 보세요. QR 코드를 스캔하면 각 알파벳과 대표 단어의 발음을 듣고 친절한 강의 영상도 시청할 수 있어요.

단모음

이제 '자음+모음+자음' 3글자로 이루어진 간단한 단어부터 읽어볼 거예요. 이미 각 글자의 소리를 알고 있으니 그 소리를 기억하며 부드럽게 이어서 발음하면 됩니다.

이중자음

이어서 모음은 그대로 하나인데 앞뒤의 자음이 두 개로 늘어나 조금 더 복잡해 보이는 단어들에 도전해 볼게요. 이중자음은 1) 각 자음의 소리를 모두 살려 부드럽게 연결하거나, 2) 둘 중 하나의 자음 소리만 남거나, 3) 전혀 다른 소리를 내기도 해요. 각각의 예시는 본문에서 상세히 다루었으니 복잡하겠다, 어렵겠다, 미리 걱정은 금물!

장모음 & 이중모음

한 걸음 더 나아가 한 단어 안에 모음이 두 개 들어 있는 단어들을 읽어 볼까요? 두 개의 모음은 자음을 사이에 두고 떨어져 있을 수도, 서로 딱 붙어 있을 수도 있어요. 중요한 것은, 한 단어에서 모음이 두 개가 되면 모음의 소리가 달라진다는 점입니다. 일반적으로 두 모음 중 앞의 모음의 '이름' 대로 소리를 내고 뒤의 모음은 소리를 내지 않는 게 규칙이고요, 이렇게 자기 이름대로 소리 나는 모음을 '장모음'이라고 해요. 한편, 두 개의 모음이 모여 새로운 소리가 되기도 하는데 이런 이중모음도 패턴 별로 상세히 다루었습니다.

기타 패턴 및 규칙

그 외에도 모음 뒤에 자음 r이 붙어 모음의 소리가 바뀌는 경우, 자음 c와 g의 두 가지 소리와 규칙, 명사의 복수형 -s와 -es의 발음, 동사의 과거/과거분사형 어미 -ed의 세 가지 발음과 규칙 등 영어 읽기 및 발음의 기본이 되는 내용들을 충실히 담았습니다.

Sight Words (사이트 워드)

또 하나. 영어에는 빈출도가 높고 문장 구성에 필수적인 Sight Words(또는 High Frequency Words)라 불리는 단어들이 있어요. the, a, it, are, I, that, said, which 등이 모두 Sight Words랍니다. 이 단어들은 파닉스 규칙으로 읽을 수 없는 것들도 있고 의미보다는 기능이 중시되므로 눈과 입에 통째로 익혀 두는 것이 좋습니다. 이 책은 매 유닛마다 파닉스 패턴 단어에 Sight Words를 더하여 만든 문장을 수록하여, 단어 읽기에서 그치지 않고 문장 읽기에까지 도전할 수 있습니다.

이렇게
학습하세요

대표소리

Aa부터 Zz까지 알파벳 26 글자의 정확한
소리를 확인하세요.

모음	**A a**	**E e**	**I i**
	cat / skate / ball	egg / see / cake	in / hi

파닉스 핵심 패턴

파닉스 패턴을 이루는 각 글자의 소리를 하
나씩 천천히 소리 내어 본 후 이어서 부드럽
게 연결하여 읽어 봅니다.

단어읽기

파닉스 패턴 앞뒤에 글자를 더하면 의미를
가진 '진짜' 단어가 됩니다. 패턴 및 각 글자
의 소리를 기억하며 단어를 읽어 보세요.

발음과 강의 듣기

QR코드를 스캔하면 해당 파닉스 패턴의 모든 음성과 선생님의
친절한 영상 강의까지 들을 수 있습니다. 절대 놓치지 마세요.

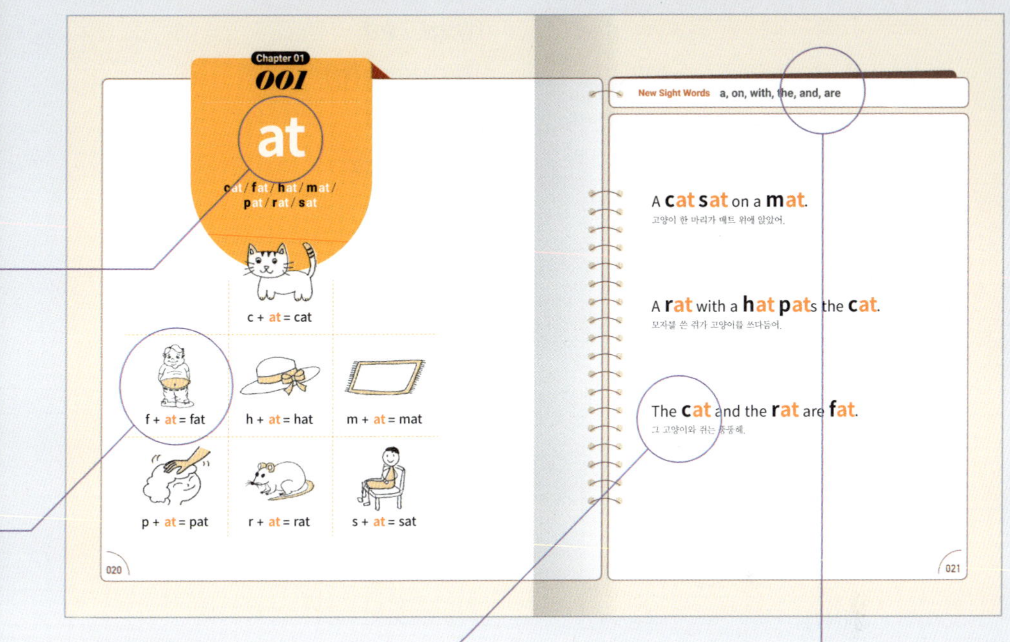

문장 읽기

파닉스 패턴 단어와 Sight Words로 이루어진
문장들을 '자신 있게' '소리 내어' 읽어 보세
요.

Sight Words (사이트 워드)

매 유닛의 문장 읽기를 도와줄 Sight Words
를 확인하세요. 단어를 보고 바로 소리 내어
읽을 수 있는지에 집중합니다.

Chapter 1
읽기의 시작, 단모음 blending!

Chapter 5

모음을 조종하는 보스, r!

Chapter 6

이것까지 알면
진짜 파닉스 다했다!

Index

아는 ABC도 다시보자!

영어알파벳 26글자의 대표소리를 알고 있나요? 확인해 보세요!

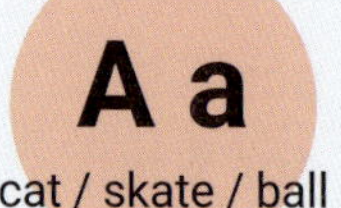

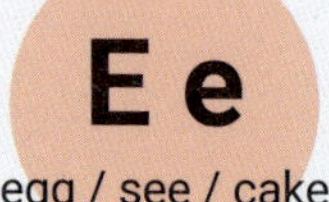

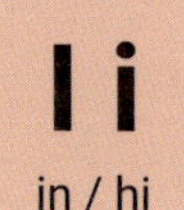

O o
hot / go / out
moon / book / boy

U u
hug / cute / rule

B b
bag

C c
can / ice

D d
dog

F f
fan

G g
game / page

H h
hat

J j
jam

K k
king

L l
like

용어 설명

단모음 단어 음절 내 모음이 하나일 때

장모음&이중모음 단어 음절 내 모음이 두 개 이상이거나 음절이 모음으로 끝날 때
두 모음은 붙어있을 수도, 떨어져 있을 수도 있음

단자음 자음 하나

이중자음 자음 두 개가 붙어 있을 때. 두 자음의 소리가 모두 나기도 하고,
둘 중 하나의 자음 소리만 나거나 전혀 새로운 소리가 나기도 함

Chapter 1

읽기의 시작,
단모음 Blending!

Blending 이란?
단어를 구성하는 각 글자의 소리를 부드럽게 이어 읽는 것을 말해요.

001

at

cat / **fat** / **hat** / **mat** /
pat / **rat** / **sat**

c + **at** = cat

f + **at** = fat

h + **at** = hat

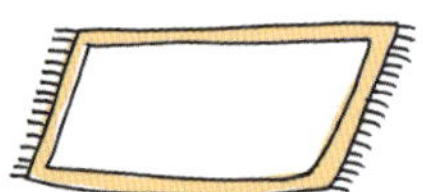

m + **at** = mat

p + **at** = pat

r + **at** = rat

s + **at** = sat

A **cat sat** on a **mat**.

고양이 한 마리가 매트 위에 앉았어.

A **rat** with a **hat pat**s the **cat**.

모자를 쓴 쥐가 고양이를 쓰다듬어.

The **cat** and the **rat** are **fat**.

그 고양이와 쥐는 뚱뚱해.

002

an

can / fan / man / pan / ran / tan / van

f + **an** = fan

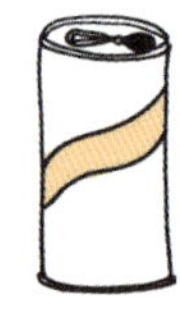

c + **an** = can

m + **an** = man

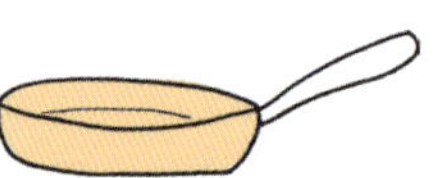

p + **an** = pan

r + **an** = ran

t + **an** = tan

v + **an** = van

The **man** with a **tan** has a **pan**.

태닝을 한 저 남자가 프라이팬을 갖고 있어.

There are a **fan** and a **can** in the **van**.

승합차 안에 부채랑 캔이 있어.

We **ran** to the **van** to get it.

우리는 그것을 가지러 승합차로 달려갔어.

003

ap

cap / lap / map / nap / rap / sap

c + **ap** = cap

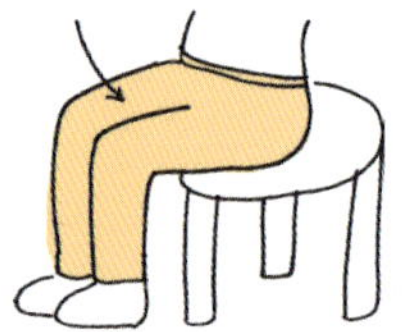

l + **ap** = lap

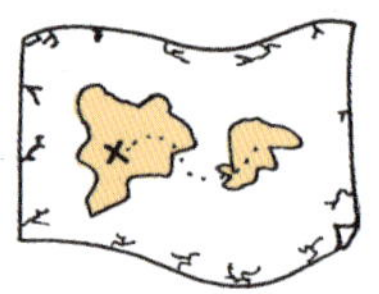

m + **ap** = map

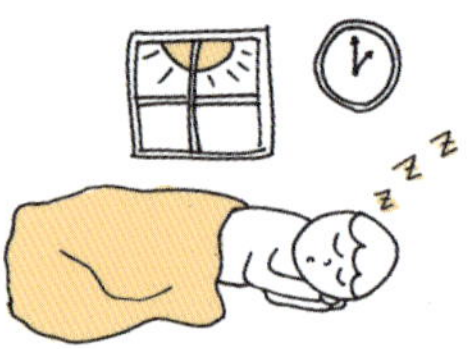

n + **ap** = nap

r + **ap** = rap

s + **ap** = sap

A **nap** on a **lap** is good.

무릎 베고 낮잠 자는 거 좋지.

The man with a **cap** can **rap**.

모자 쓴 저 남자 랩 좀 하네.

I need a **map** to find the **sap**.

수액을 찾으려면 지도가 필요해.

004

ag

bag / **n**ag / **r**ag / **t**ag / **w**ag

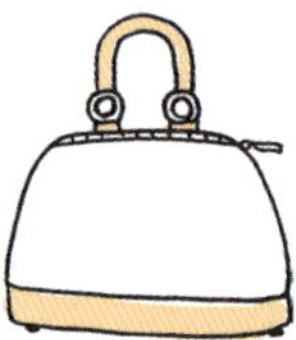

b + **ag** = bag

n + **ag** = nag

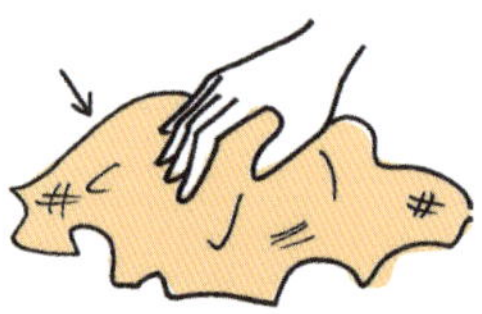

r + **ag** = rag

t + **ag** = tag

w + **ag** = wag

Cats do not **wag**.

고양이는 꼬리 치지 않지.

I have a **bag** with a **tag**.

나는 꼬리표가 달린 가방이 있어.

Do not **nag** about the **rag**!

그 행주 가지고 잔소리 하지 마!

005

ad(d)

add / **bad** / **dad** / **lad** / **mad** / **pad** / **sad**

add

b + **ad** = bad

d + **ad** = dad

l + **ad** = lad

m + **ad** = mad

p + **ad** = pad

s + **ad** = sad

The **bad lad** is **sad**.

그 나쁜 녀석이 슬퍼하고 있어.

Dad can **add** the **pad**.

아빠가 메모지를 추가로 넣으면 되잖아.

Dad was **mad** at the **bad lad**.

아빠는 그 나쁜 녀석에게 화가 났어.

006

ab

cab / **dab** / **fab** / **jab** /
lab / **tab**

c + **ab** = cab

d + **ab** = dab

f + **ab** = fab

j + **ab** = jab

l + **ab** = lab

t + **ab** = tab

Dab it on the **tab**.

그걸 그 색인표에 살살 발라봐.

The **fab cab** was made in a **lab**.

그 멋진 택시는 실험실에서 만들어졌어.

Did you **jab** the man in the **cab**?

네가 택시에 있는 그 남자를 쿡쿡 찔렀어?

007

am

bam / **dam** / **ham** / **jam** /
ram / **yam**

b + **am** = bam

d + **am** = dam

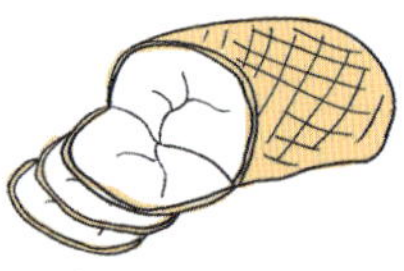

h + **am** = ham

j + **am** = jam

r + **am** = ram

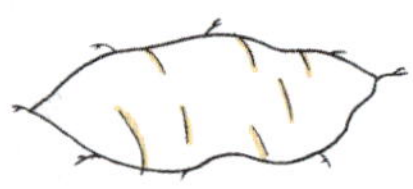

y + **am** = yam

I like **jam** on a **yam**.

난 마에다가 잼 발라 먹는 거 좋아해.

Put the **ham** on the pan.

프라이팬에다가 햄을 올려.

Bam! Did the cab just **ram** the **dam**?

쾅! 지금 저 택시가 댐을 들이받은 거야?

008

ack

**back / pack / rack /
sack / tack**

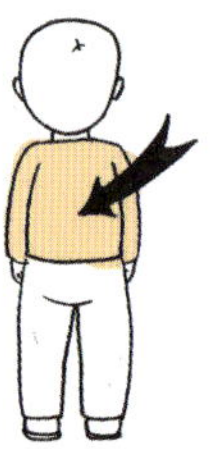

b + **ack** = back

p + **ack** = pack

r + **ack** = rack

s + **ack** = sack

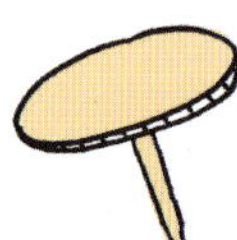

t + **ack** = tack

I don't like to **pack**.

나 짐 싸는 거 안 좋아해.

Put the **sack** on the **rack**.

자루는 그 신반에 올려놔.

Oh! I got a **tack** in my **back**!

앗! 내 등에 압정이 꽂혀 있어!

009

ig

big / **d**ig / **f**ig / **j**ig /
pig / **w**ig

b + **ig** = big

d + **ig** = dig

f + **ig** = fig

j + **ig** = jig

p + **ig** = pig

w + **ig** = wig

The **big pig** can **dig**.

저 큰 돼지가 땅을 잘 파네.

I can **jig** with the **wig** on.

나는 가발 쓰고 춤 잘 춰.

Dig out the **big fig**.

그 큰 무화과를 파내.

010

it(t)

bit / **f**it / **h**it / **k**it /
mitt / **s**it

b + **it** = bit

f + **it** = fit

h + **it** = hit

k + **it** = kit

m + **itt** = mitt

s + **it** = sit

Do not **sit** on the **mitt**.

장갑 위에 앉지 마.

Does it **fit** or is it a **bit** big?

그거 딱 맞아 아니면 좀 커?

I **hit** the **kit** as I ran out.

내가 달려 나가다가 그 키트를 쳤어.

011

ip

dip / **hip** / **lip** / **rip** / **sip** / **tip** / **zip**

z + **ip** = zip

d + **ip** = dip

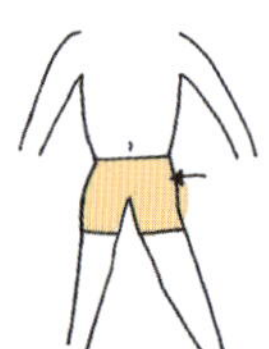

h + **ip** = hip

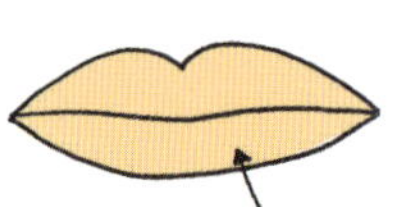

l + **ip** = lip

r + **ip** = rip

s + **ip** = sip

t + **ip** = tip

Rip the **z**ip!

그 지퍼 뜯어버려!

Tip it and have a **s**ip.

그걸 기울여서 조금 마셔.

I hit my **lip** and **hip** as I ran for a **dip**.

수영하러 뛰어가다 입술이랑 엉덩이를 부딪혔어.

012

id

bid / **h**id / **k**id / **l**id / **r**id

b + **id** = bid

h + **id** = hid

k + **id** = kid

l + **id** = lid

r + **id** = rid

Did you get **rid** of the **lid**?

너 그 뚜껑 버렸어?

The **kid hid** under the **lid**.

그 꼬마는 뚜껑 아래에 숨었어.

I did not **bid** for you. I did it for the **kid**.

널 위해 입찰한 게 아니야. 그 꼬마를 위해서 한 거야.

013

in(n)

inn / **b**in / **d**in / **f**in / **k**in /
pin / **t**in / **w**in

inn

b + in = bin

d + in = din

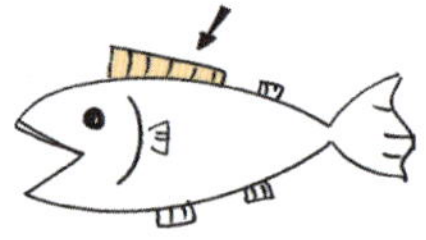

f + in = fin

k + in = kin

p + in = pin

t + in = tin

w + in = win

The **tin bin** made a **din**.

그 금속 쓰레기통이 시끄러운 소리를 냈어.

I'll **win** the **pin** with the **fin**.

나는 그 지느러미가 달린 핀을 받고 말 거야!

My **kin** isn't in the **inn**.

내 친척은 그 여관에 없어.

014

ick

kick / **lick** / **pick** / **sick** / **tick** / **wick**

k + **ick** = kick

l + **ick** = lick

p + **ick** = pick

s + **ick** = sick

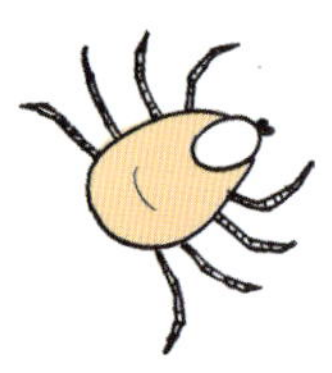

t + **ick** = tick

w + **ick** = wick

Pick up the **tick** and **kick** it into the bin.

진드기를 집어서 발로 차 쓰레기통에 넣어.

Don't **lick** it. You will get **sick**.

그거 핥지마. 병 걸려.

Did you **pick** the **wick** you like?

마음에 드는 심지를 고르셨나요?

015

og

bog / dog / fog / hog / jog / log

b + **og** = bog

d + **og** = dog

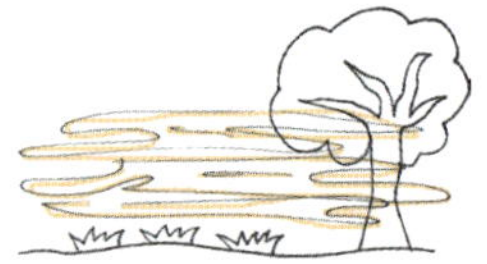

f + **og** = fog

h + **og** = hog

j + **og** = jog

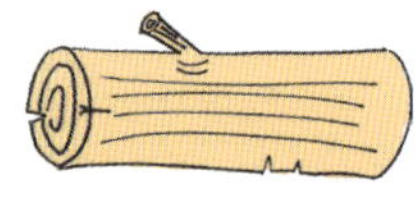

l + **og** = log

Get the **dog** out of the **bog**!

개를 늪에서 건져 내!

There is too much **fog** to go for a **jog**.

조깅하러 가기에는 안개가 너무 많아.

Is that a **hog** on the **log**?

저 통나무 위에 있는 저거 돼지야?

016

op

cop / **h**op / **m**op / **p**op / **s**op / **t**op

c + **op** = cop

h + **op** = hop

m + **op** = mop

p + **op** = pop

s + **op** = sop

t + **op** = top

Sop it up with a **m**op.

걸레로 빨아들여.

The **cop**s **hop** here and there.

경찰들이 여기저기 바쁘게 다니네.

Pop! A **top** came out of the hat!

펑! 모자에서 팽이가 나왔네!

017

ot

dot / hot / lot / not /
pot / tot

d + **ot** = dot

h + **ot** = hot

l + **ot** = lot

n + **ot** = not

p + **ot** = pot

t + **ot** = tot

There is some ham in the **hot pot**.

뜨거운 국물에 햄이 좀 들어 있어.

A **lot** of **dot**s are on the **tot**.

꼬마 몸에 동그란 점 무늬가 많이 있네.

I got mad, **not** sad.

난 슬픈 게 아니라 화가 났던 거야.

018

ob

cob / **job** / **mob** / **rob** / **sob**

c + **ob** = cob

j + **ob** = job

m + **ob** = mob

r + **ob** = rob

s + **ob** = sob

The **mob** looks really mad.

저 사람들 엄청 화난 것 같은데.

They want to **rob** the **cob**s.

저 사람들이 옥수수를 훔치려고 해.

Your **job** is just to **sob**.

네가 할 일은 그냥 우는 것뿐이야.

019

od(d)

odd / **cod** / **god** / **nod** /
pod / **rod**

odd

c + **od** = cod

g + **od** = god

n + **od** = nod

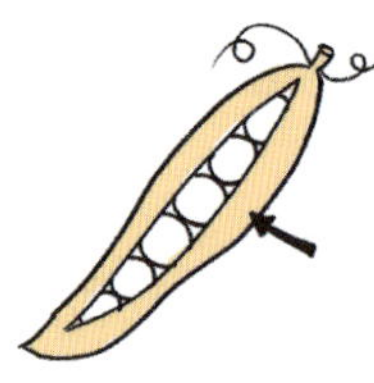

p + **od** = pod

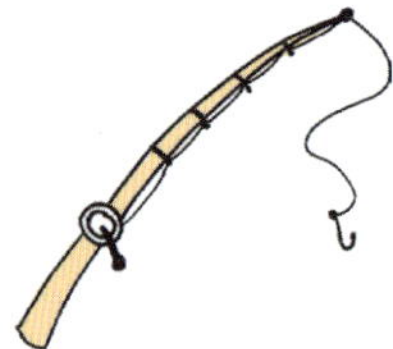

r + **od** = rod

There was a **cod** on the **rod**.

낚싯대에 대구가 걸려 있었어.

The **cod** on the **rod** had a **pod**.

낚싯대에 걸린 대구가 콩 꼬투리를 물고 있더라.

God will even **nod** on the **odd**.

하나님은 이상한 자들조차 굽어살피신다.

020

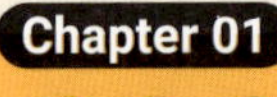

ock

dock / **l**ock / **m**ock /
rock / **s**ock

d + **ock** = dock

l + **ock** = lock

m + **ock** = mock

r + **ock** = rock

s + **ock** = sock

Where are my **sock**s and **lock**s?

내 양말이랑 자물쇠 어디 있어?

Don't **mock** me!

나 놀리지 마!

The **dock** is on a **rock**.

그 부두는 바위 위에 있어.

021

en

den / hen / men / pen / ten / yen

d + **en** = den

h + **en** = hen

m + **en** = men

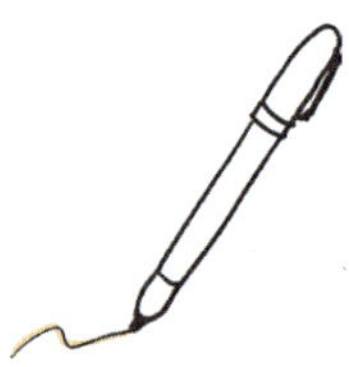

p + **en** = pen

t + **en** = ten

y + **en** = yen

The pen is ten yen.
그 펜은 10엔(¥)이야.

The men all want the big hen.
그 사람들은 모두 그 큰 암탉을 원해.

The hen is in the den.
그 암탉은 굴 안에 있어.

022

et

get / jet / met / net / pet / set / vet / wet

g + **et** = get

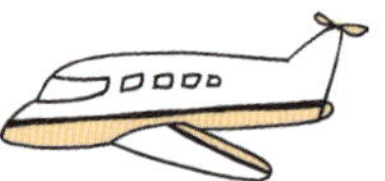

j + **et** = jet

m + **et** = met

n + **et** = net

p + **et** = pet

s + **et** = set

v + **et** = vet

w + **et** = wet

Let the **jet set** off!

제트기 출발시켜!

The **vet met** the **wet pet**.

그 수의사는 물에 젖은 애완견을 만났다.

Don't **get** the **net** yet.

아직 그물 가져오지 마.

023

ed

bed / **f**ed / **l**ed / **r**ed / **T**ed

b + **ed** = bed

f + **ed** = fed

l + **ed** = led

r + **ed** = red

T + **ed** = Ted

He **led** me to the dock.

그는 나를 부두로 안내했다.

I'm **fed** up with the **red** jam!

난 그 빨간 잼이라면 지긋지긋해!

Ted is still in **bed**.

테드는 아직 안 일어났어.

024

eg(g)

egg / beg / keg / leg / peg

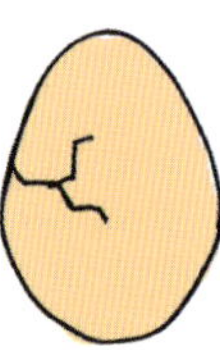

egg

b + **eg** = beg

k + **eg** = keg

l + **eg** = leg

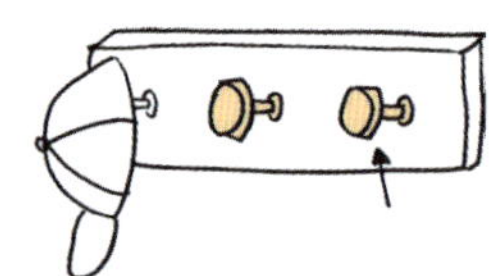

p + **eg** = peg

I hit my **leg** against a **keg**.

나는 맥주 통에 다리를 부딪쳤어.

The **egg**s are under the **peg**s.

달걀은 말뚝 아래에 있어.

I **beg** for an **egg**.

제발 달걀 하나만 주세요.

025

ell

bell / **f**ell / **s**ell / **t**ell / **w**ell / **y**ell

b + **ell** = bell

f + **ell** = fell

s + **ell** = sell

t + **ell** = tell

w + **ell** = well

y + **ell** = yell

I will **tell** them to pack the **b**ell**s**.

내가 그 사람들한테 종을 포장하라고 할게.

"**B**ell**s**! We **sell** **b**ell**s**!" they **y**ell.

"종이요! 종 팔아요!" 그들은 소리쳐.

The **b**ell**s** **f**ell into the **w**ell.

종들이 우물에 빠져 버렸어.

026

eck

deck / **n**eck / **p**eck

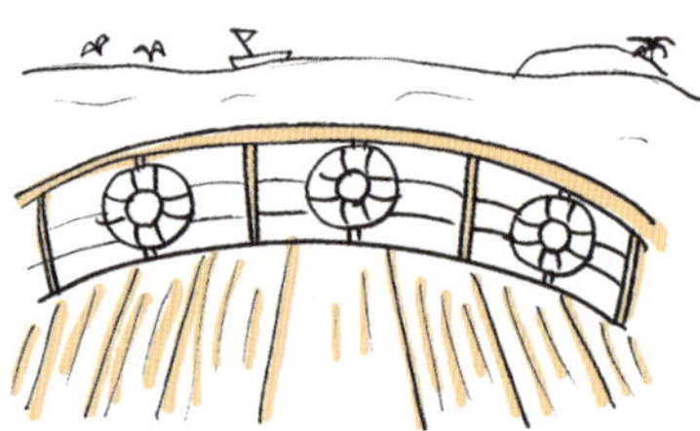

d + **eck** = deck

n + **eck** = neck

p + **eck** = peck

The dogs are on the **deck**.

개들은 갑판에 있어.

Neck and **neck**! Who is going to win?

막상막하하네요! 누가 이길까요?

I got a **peck** on my lips.

나는 입술에 가벼운 키스를 받았어.

027

ub

cub / **dub** / **hub** / **pub** /
rub / **sub** / **tub**

c + **ub** = cub

d + **ub** = dub

h + **ub** = hub

p + **ub** = pub

r + **ub** = rub

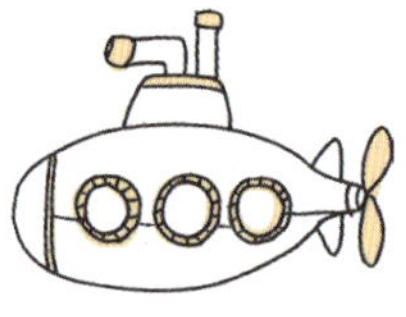

s + **ub** = sub

t + **ub** = tub

The **cub**s like to **rub** in the **tub**.

그 아기곰들은 욕조에서 목욕하는 걸 좋아해.

You can get to the **hub** by **sub**.

중심부까지는 잠수함을 타고 갈 수 있습니다.

He always goes to the **pub** after he **dub**s.

그는 더빙 후에는 항상 술집에 간다.

028

ug

bug / dug / hug / jug /
mug / pug / rug / tug

b + **ug** = bug

d + **ug** = dug

h + **ug** = hug

j + **ug** = jug

m + **ug** = mug

p + **ug** = pug

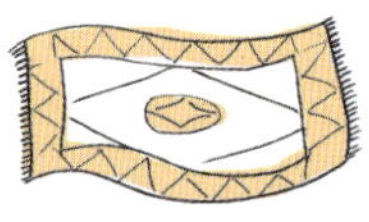

r + **ug** = rug

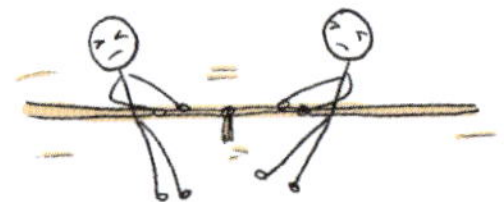

t + **ug** = tug

The **pug dug** the **jug** out.

그 퍼그는 그 주전자를 캐냈다.

The **bug**s **tug** the **rug** to get the **mug**.

벌레들이 컵을 손에 넣으려고 깔개를 당겨.

I will **hug** the **pug**. Help me put it on the **rug**.

내가 그 퍼그를 안을 게. 퍼그를 카펫에 올려 놓는 걸 도와 줘.

029

ut(t)

butt / **g**ut / **h**ut / **m**utt /
nut / **p**utt / **r**ut

b + **utt** = butt

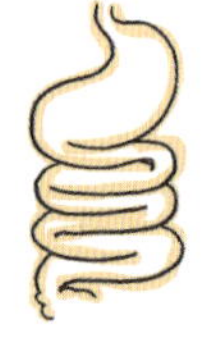

g + **ut** = gut

h + **ut** = hut

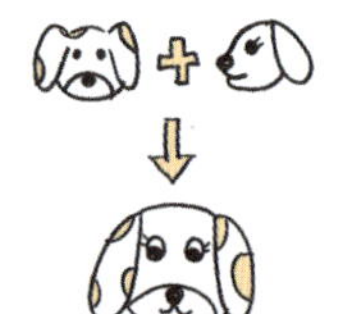

m + **utt** = mutt

n + **ut** = nut

p + **utt** = putt

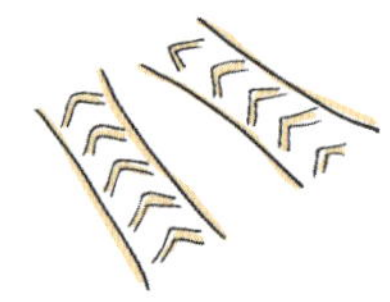

r + **ut** = rut

Get your **butt** over here to the **hut**!

당장 이리로 와서 오두막으로 가!

I don't have the **gut**s to **putt** here.

난 여기서 퍼팅할 배짱은 없는데.

The **mutt** can get the **nut** from the **rut**.

그 개가 바퀴 자국에서 호두를 꺼낼 수 있을 거야.

030

un

bun / **d**un / **g**un / **n**un /
run / **s**un

b + **un** = bun

d + **un** = dun

g + **un** = gun

n + **un** = nun

r + **un** = run

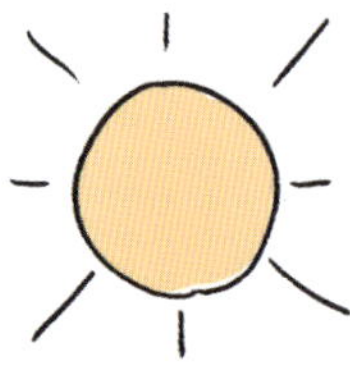

s + **un** = sun

He would **run** with the **gun**.
그는 그 총을 가지고 도망갈 거야.

The **nun** put the **bun**s under the **sun**.
그 수녀는 빵들을 햇볕에 내놓았다.

The **bun**s became **dun**.
빵들이 회갈색이 되었네.

031

up

up / **p**up / **t**up / **y**up

up

p + up = pup

t + up = tup

y + up = yup

Did the **p****up** go **up**?

강아지가 올라갔어?

Y**up**, it did. And it went after a **t****up**.

응. 그리고는 숫양을 쫓아갔어.

A **t****up** and a **p****up** don't get along.

숫양이랑 강아지는 사이가 좋지 않은데.

032

uck

buck / **d**uck / **l**uck / **s**uck / **t**uck / **y**uck

b + **uck** = buck

d + **uck** = duck

l + **uck** = luck

s + **uck** = suck

t + **uck** = tuck

y + **uck** = yuck

It **suck**s up everything. **Yuck**!

그건 모든 것을 빨아들여. 으윅!

The **duck** has no **luck** with the **buck**.

그 오리는 수사슴이랑은 상대가 안 돼.

Can you **tuck** the **duck** under the bed?

그 오리 좀 침대 아래로 밀어 넣어 줄래?

033

-X

ax / fax / tax / fix / mix / box

ax

f + ax = fax

t + ax = tax

f + ix = fix

m + ix = mix

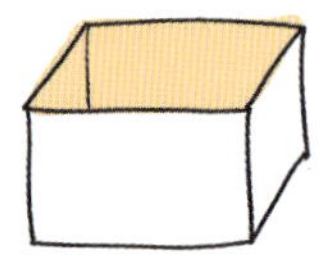

b + ox = box

The **ax** is in the **box**.
도끼는 그 상자 안에 있어요.

Do not **mix** it. **Fix** it.
섞지 말고 고정을 시키라고.

Fax him that the **tax** went up.
그 사람한테 세금이 올랐다고 팩스 좀 보내.

034

-S [1]

cats / rats / sacks / mitts / socks / pups / nuts

cat / cat**s**

rat / rat**s**

sack / sack**s**

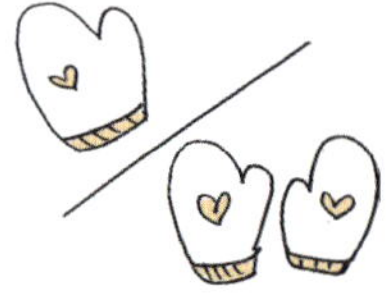

mitt / mitt**s**

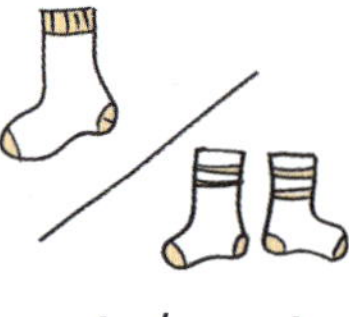

sock / sock**s**

pup / pup**s**

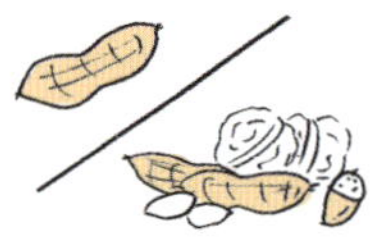

nut / nut**s**

Do you want **socks** or **mitts**?

양말이 좋아? 벙어리 장갑이 좋아?

Cats like **rats**, not **pups**.

고양이는 강아지가 아니라 쥐를 좋아하지.

Take the **nuts** out of the **sacks**.

자루에서 견과들 좀 꺼내.

035

-S②

bags / tags / kids / dogs / logs / eggs / buns

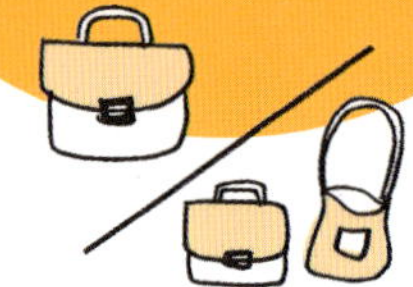

bag / bags

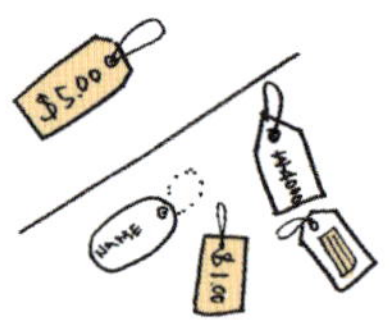

tag / tags

kid / kids

dog / dogs

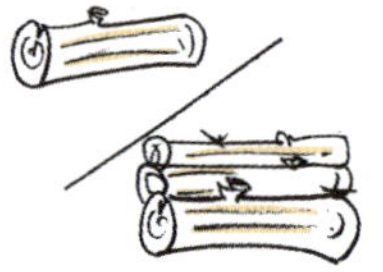

log / logs

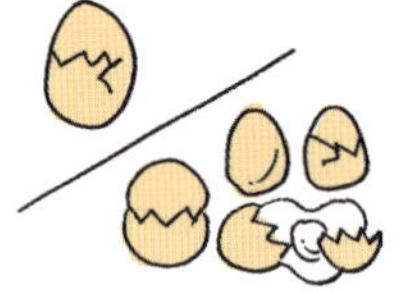

egg / eggs

bun / buns

Put the **eggs** on the **buns**.

달걀을 빵 위에 올리세요.

Look at the **dogs** on the **logs**!

통나무 위에 있는 개들 좀 봐!

The **kids** have **bags** with **tags**.

아이들이 가격표가 달린 가방을 메고 있어.

Chapter 2

따로 또 같이,
이중자음

자음 두 개가 붙어있는 이중자음에는 1) 두 자음의 소리를 그대로 이어 읽는 것과
2) 그냥 하나의 소리로 발음하는 것, 두 종류가 있어요.

036

st-

stack / **st**em / **st**ep / **st**ick / **st**op / **st**uck / **st**ud

st + ack = stack

st + em = stem

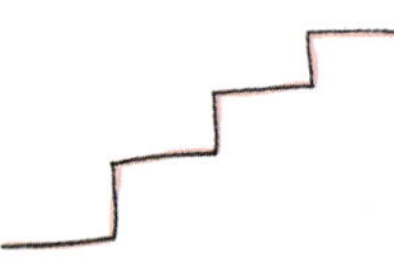

st + ep = step

st + ick = stick

st + op = stop

st + uck = stuck

st + ud = stud

Oh! The **stud**s are **stuck**.

아! 징들이 끼었어.

Put the **stem**s on the **step**s.

줄기들은 계단 위에 둬.

St op! Don't **stack** any more **stick**s!

그만! 막대 그만 쌓아!

037

sm-

smack / smell / smock / smog / smug

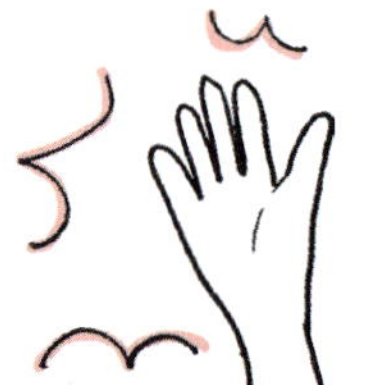

sm + ack = smack

sm + ell = smell

sm + ock = smock

sm + og = smog

sm + ug = smug

That **smock** is a bit big for her.

그 작업복은 그녀에게는 좀 커.

What a lot of **smog**! I can even **smell** it.

매연이 너무 많아! 냄새를 맡을 수 있을 정도야.

What is he so **smug** about?
Oh, I want to **smack** him on the back!

저 자식은 뭐 때문에 저렇게 의기양양해 하는 거야? 아, 저 자식 등 한 대 갈기고 싶다!

038

sn-

snack / **sn**iff / **sn**ip / **sn**ob / **sn**ot

sn + ack = snack

sn + iff = sniff

sn + ip = snip

sn + ob = snob

sn + ot = snot

Sn**iff**! Sn**iff**!
- Yuck! Your **sn**ot is out!

훌쩍! 훌쩍! – 으웩! 너 콧물 나왔어!

Don't give him a **sn**ack. He's a **sn**ob.

쟤는 간식 주지 마. 잘난 척 쟁이야.

How do you open the **sn**ack bags?
- Just **sn**ip them.

과장 봉지 어떻게 뜯어? – 그냥 가위로 잘라.

039

sp-

speck / **sp**ed / **sp**ill / **sp**in / **sp**it / **sp**ot

sp + eck = speck

sp + ed = sped

sp + ill = spill

sp + in = spin

sp + it = spit

sp + ot = spot

Don't **sp**in it. Or you will **sp**ill it.

그거 돌리지 마. 안 그러면 쏟는다.

Your **sp**it made **sp**ots on the rug!

네 침이 카펫에 얼룩을 만들었잖아!

He **sp**ed away and now he is just a **sp**eck.

서둘러 가더니 그는 이제 작은 점처럼 보여.

040

SW-

swam / **sw**ell / **sw**im / **Sw**iss

sw + am = swam

sw + ell = swell

sw + im = swim

Sw + iss = Swiss

Can you **swim**?

수영할 줄 알아?

Did you hit your leg? It's about to **swell** up!

너 다리 부딪쳤어? 부으려고 해!

That **Swiss** man **swam** all the way here!

저 스위스 남자가 헤엄쳐서 여기까지나 왔대!

041

sc- & sk-

scab / **sc**an / **sc**off / **sc**um / **sk**im / **sk**ull

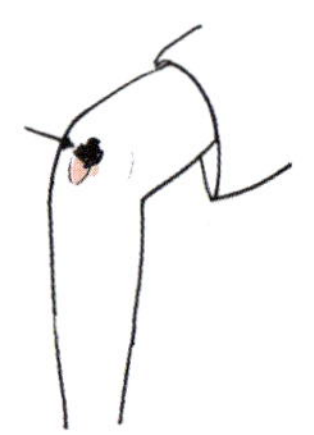

sc + ab = scab

sc + an = scan

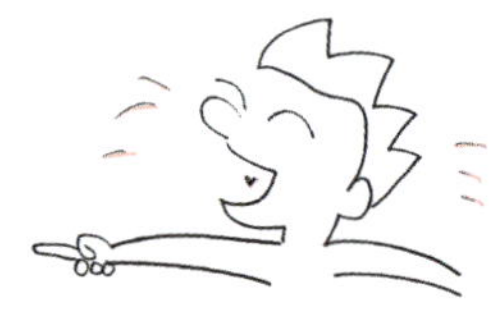

sc + off = scoff

sc + um = scum

sk + im = skim

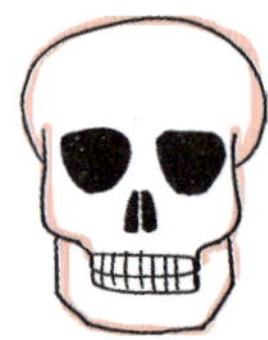

sk + ull = skull

They want to **scan** his **skull**.

그들은 그의 두개골을 정밀 검사하고 싶어 해.

Skim the **sc**um off.

거품을 걷어내.

He will **scoff** and say, "It's only a **scab**."

그 사람은 비웃으며 "그건 그냥 딱지일 뿐이잖아."라고 말할걸.

042

bl-

black / **bl**eb / **bl**ed / **bl**ob /
block / **bl**uff

bl + ack = black

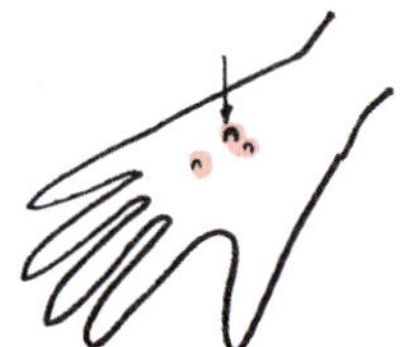

bl + eb = bleb

bl + ed = bled

bl + ob = blob

bl + ock = block

bl + uff = bluff

What's that **black blob**?

그 검은색 물방울은 뭐야?

Don't pop the **bleb**. I once did and it **bled**.

물집 터뜨리지 마. 나 예전에 한 번 터뜨렸었는데 피 났어.

He likes to **bluff** about how many **block**s he has.

걔는 자기가 블록을 얼마나 많이 가졌는지 허풍 떠는 걸 좋아해.

043

cl-

clack / **cl**am / **cl**an / **cl**ass /
cliff / **cl**ock / **cl**ub / **cl**uck

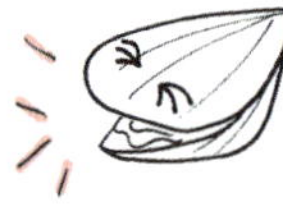

cl + ack = clack

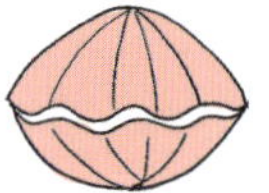

cl + am = clam

cl + an = clan

cl + ass = class

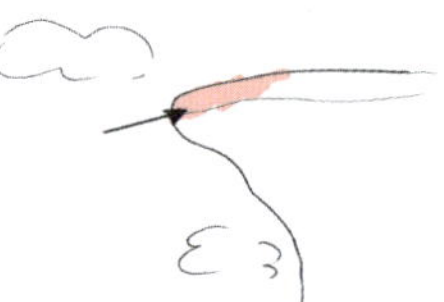

cl + iff = cliff

cl + ock = clock

cl + ub = club

cl + uck = cluck

Let's go see the **club** after **class**.

학교 마치고 그 클럽 보러 가자.

The **clam**s **clack** and the hens **cluck**.

조개들은 딱딱거리고 암탉들은 꼬꼬댁거려.

The **clan** found the **clock** on a **cliff**.

그 무리는 절벽에서 그 시계를 찾아냈다.

044

fl-

flag / **fl**ap / **fl**at / **fl**eck /
flick / **fl**ip / **fl**oss

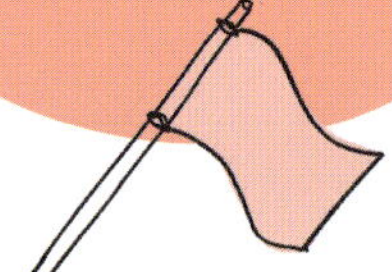

fl + ag = flag

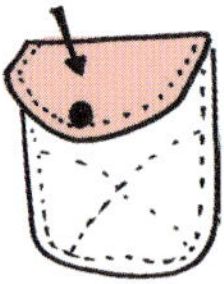

fl + ap = flap

fl + at = flat

fl + eck = fleck

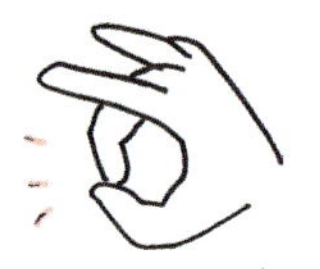

fl + ick = flick

fl + ip = flip

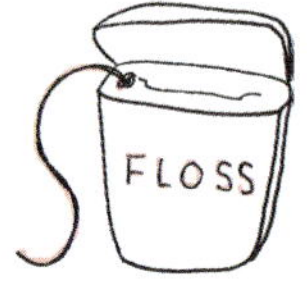

fl + oss = floss

Did the children **flip** the **flag**?

아이들이 그 깃발을 뒤집었니?

Get the **floss** out of the **flat flap**.

그 납작한 덮개에서 치실을 꺼내.

Flick the **fleck**s off the hat.

모자에 붙은 부스러기들을 손으로 튕겨 내.

045

gl-

glad / **glam** / **glass** /
gloss / **glum**

gl + ad = glad

gl + am = glam

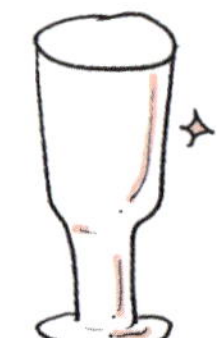

gl + ass = glass

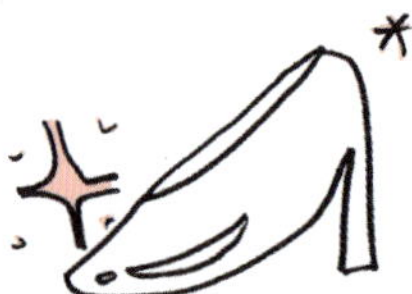

gl + oss = gloss

gl + um = glum

How do you always look so **glam**?
너는 어떻게 항상 그렇게 멋지냐?

This lipstick gives a **gloss** like **glass**.
이 립스틱은 유리 같은 광택을 선사합니다.

Why are you so **glum**?
– I'm not **glum**. I'm **glad**!
너 왜 그렇게 우울해? – 나 안 우울한데? 나 기분 좋아!

046

pl-

plan / **pl**od / **pl**op / **pl**uck / **pl**ug / **pl**um / **pl**us

pl + an = plan

pl + od = plod

pl + op = plop

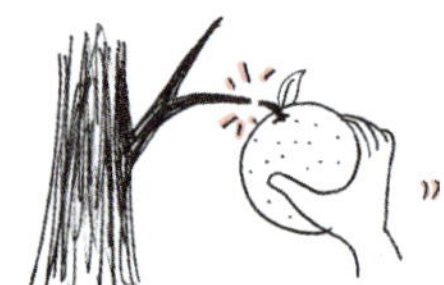

pl + uck = pluck

pl + ug = plug

pl + um = plum

pl + us = plus

I have a **pl**an. Let's **pl**u**g** it in.

나한테 계획이 있어. 플러그를 꽂자.

Plus, we'll have to **pl**od on.
– No!

게다가, 우린 계속 걸어가야 해. – 안돼!

You can **pl**uck the **pl**ums and **pl**op them into the pot.

자두를 따서 냄비에 던져 넣으면 돼.

047

sl-

slam / **sl**ed / **sl**id / **sl**im / **sl**ip / **sl**it / **sl**ot / **sl**ug

sl + am = slam

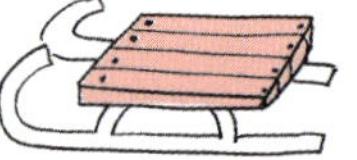

sl + ed = sled

sl + id = slid

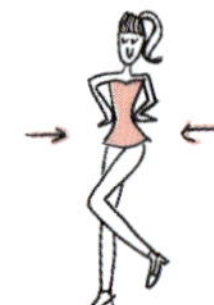

sl + im = slim

sl + ip = slip

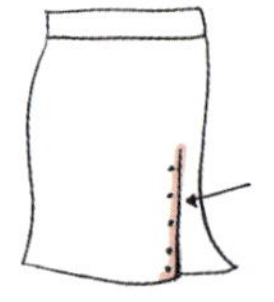

sl + it = slit

sl + ot = slot

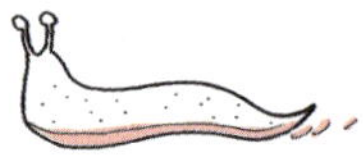

sl + ug = slug

The **slim slug slid** down like a **sled**.
그 날씬한 민달팽이는 썰매처럼 미끄러져 내려갔다.

I put it in the **slot** and it gave a **slam**.
내가 그것을 구멍에 넣자 그것은 쾅 하는 소리를 냈다.

What are those **slit**s for?
- We'll **slip** through them.
저 틈들은 왜 있는 거야? – 우리가 그 사이로 빠져 나갈 거야.

048

br-

brag / bran / brass / brat / brick / brig / brim

br + ag = brag

br + an = bran

br + ass = brass

br + at = brat

br + ick = brick

br + ig = brig

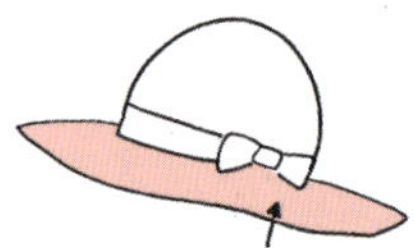

br + im = brim

The **br**at wants to have some **br**an.

그 버릇없는 아이는 겨를 좀 먹고 싶대.

She **br**ags about her hat with a **br**im.

그녀는 자신의 챙모자를 자랑해.

That **br**ig is made of **br**ass and **br**icks.

저 범선은 놋쇠랑 벽돌로 만들어졌어.

049

cr-

crab / **cr**ack / **cr**am / **cr**ib / **cr**op

cr + ab = crab

cr + ack = crack

cr + am = cram

cr + ib = crib

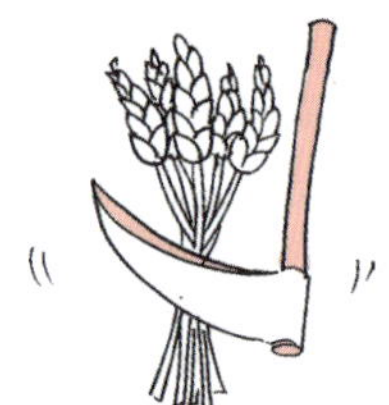

cr + op = crop

Cram the **crop** in the sack.
수확한 걸 자루에다 눌러 담아.

There is a little **crab** in the **crib**.
아기 침대에 작은 게가 있어.

Do you see the **crack**s in the **crib**?
아기 침대에 금 간 거 보여?

050

dr-

drag / **dr**ess / **dr**ill / **dr**ip / **dr**op / **dr**um

dr + ag = drag

dr + ess = dress

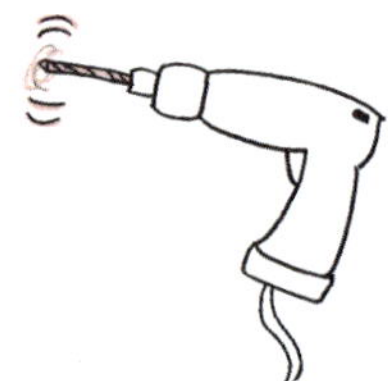

dr + ill = drill

dr + ip = drip

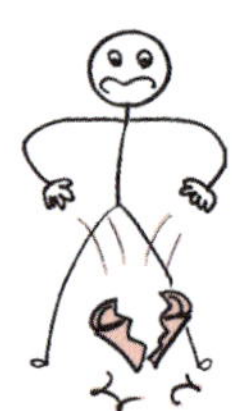

dr + op = drop

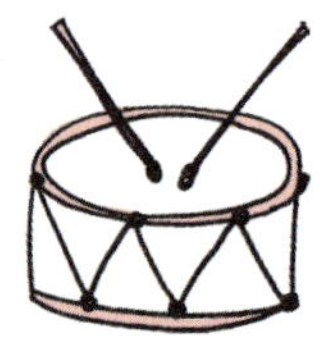

dr + um = drum

Hit the **drum**s, not **drop** them!

드럼을 치라고, 떨어트리지 말고!

The **drip**s fell onto the **dress**.

물방울들이 원피스 위로 떨어졌다.

Did you **drag** that big **drill** all by yourself?

그 큰 드릴을 너 혼자 끌고 갔다고?

051

fr-

fret / frill / frizz / frock / frog

+ et = fret

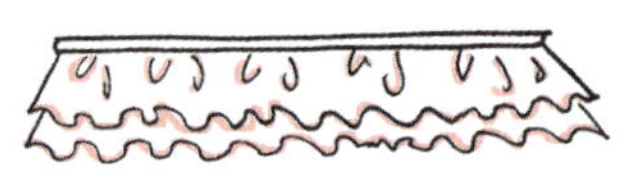

+ ill = frill

fr + izz = frizz

fr + ock = frock

fr + og = frog

Where is Mrs. **Frog** from?

개구리 아줌마는 어디서 온 거야?

The **frock** has no **frill**s at all.

그 드레스는 주름 장식이 하나도 없잖아.

Don't **fret** about the **frizz**. I'll fix it.

머리 곱슬곱슬한 건 걱정하지 마. 내가 다듬어 줄게.

052

gr-

gran / **gr**ass / **gr**ill / **gr**in / **gr**ub

gr + an = gran

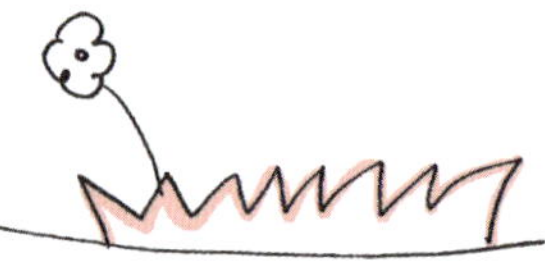

gr + ass = grass

gr + ill = grill

gr + in = grin

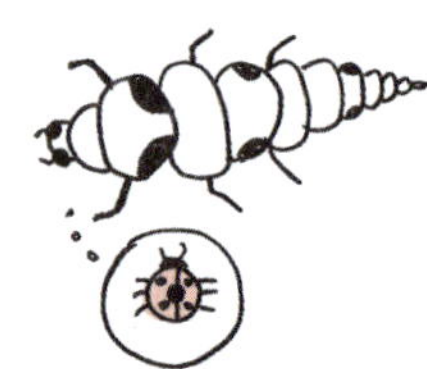

gr + ub = grub

There's a **grub** on the **grass**.

잔디 위에 무당벌레 유충이 있어.

Gran grins a lot.

할머니는 미소를 잘 지으셔.

There is **grass** stuck on the **grill**.

그릴에 풀이 껴 있어.

053

pr-

pram / **pr**ess / **pr**ick / **pr**od / **pr**om

pr + am = pram

pr + ess = press

pr + ick = prick

pr + od = prod

pr + om = prom

This is my dress for the **pr**om.

이게 내 졸업 파티 드레스야.

Press it and the **pr**am will come out.

그걸 누르면 유모차가 나올 거야.

Don't **pr**ick or **pr**od anyone.

다른 사람을 찌르거나 쑤시지 마세요.

054

tr-

tram / **tr**ap / **tr**ick / **tr**ip / **tr**oll / **tr**uck

tr + am = tram

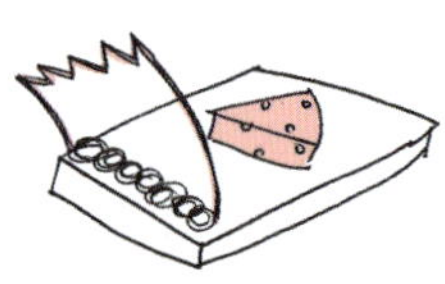

tr + ap = trap

tr + ick = trick

tr + ip = trip

tr + oll = troll

tr + uck = truck

A rat is on the **truck**! Get me a **trap** now!

트럭 위에 쥐가 있잖아! 덫 좀 빨리 갖다줘!

Did you see his **trick**s with a **troll**?

그 사람이 괴물이랑 하는 마술 봤어?

I'm going on a **trip**. I'll take the **tram** this time.

나 여행 갈 건데, 이번에는 전차 타고 갈 거야.

055

ch-

**chat / check / chick / chill /
chin / chip / chop**

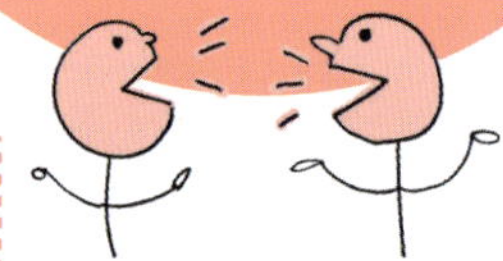

ch + at = chat

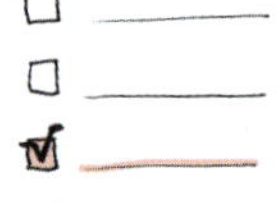

ch + eck = check

ch + ick = chick

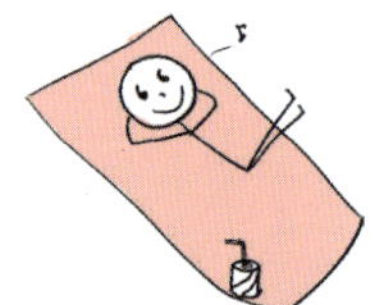

ch + ill = chill

ch + in = chin

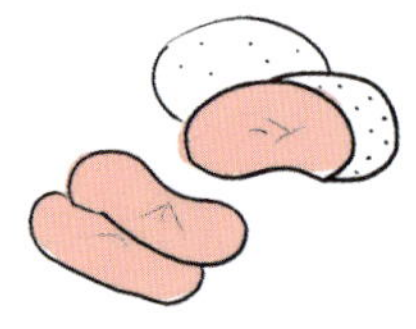

ch + ip = chip

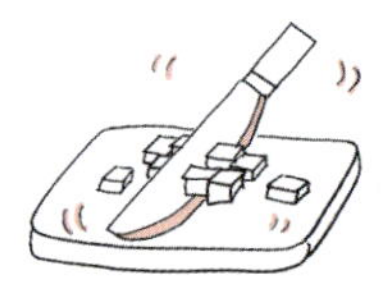

ch + op = chop

Chill out. It's only a **ch**ick.

진정해. 그냥 병아리일 뿐이야.

Don't **ch**at when you **ch**op.

칼질할 때는 잡담하지 마.

You got some **ch**ips on your **ch**in.
Go **ch**eck it.

턱에 과자 묻었다. 가서 봐봐.

056

sh-

shell / **sh**in / **sh**ip / **sh**ock / **sh**op / **sh**ot / **sh**ut

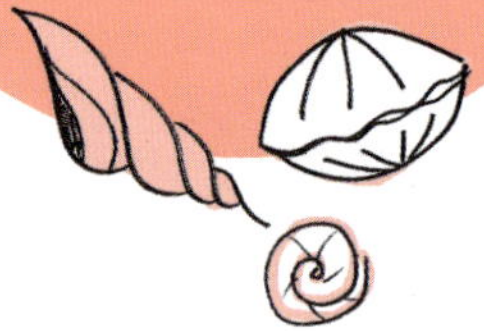

sh + ell = shell

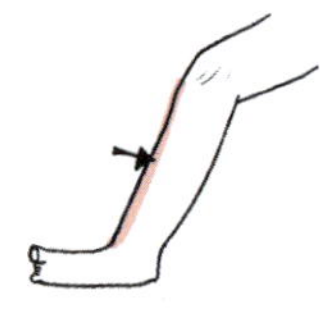

sh + in = shin

sh + ip = ship

sh + ock = shock

sh + op = shop

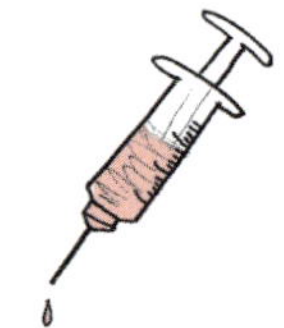

sh + ot = shot

sh + ut = shut

She found a big **shell** on the **ship**.

그녀는 배에서 큰 조개껍데기를 찾아냈다.

The **shop** was already **shut** when we got there.

우리가 갔을 때 그 가게는 이미 닫혀 있었다.

It came as a **shock** that I had to get a **shot** in the **shin**.

정강이에 주사를 맞아야 된다는 사실은 내게 충격이었다.

057

wh-

whack / **wh**am / **wh**en /
whiff / **wh**im / **wh**ip

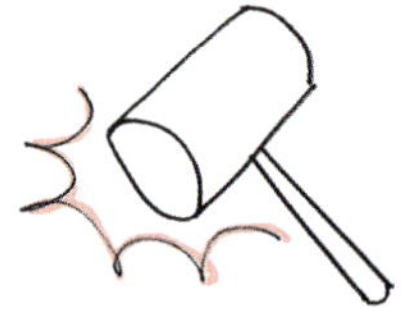

wh + ack = whack

wh + am = wham

wh + en = when

wh + iff = whiff

wh + im = whim

wh + ip = whip

Wham! And there was a **wh**iff of smog.
쿵! 그리고는 매연 냄새가 훅 풍겼다.

Until **wh**en do I have to **wh**ip the eggs?
언제까지 달걀을 휘젓고 있어야 해?

He sometimes **wh**acks things on a **wh**im.
그는 가끔 충동적으로 물건들을 세게 내리치곤 한다.

058

th-①

thick / **th**in / **th**ud / **th**ug

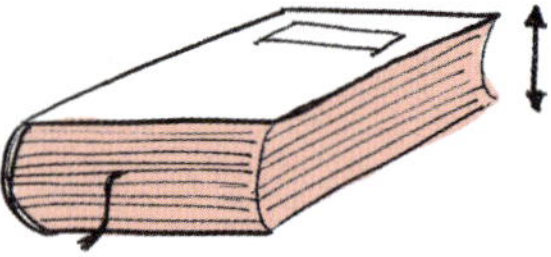

th + ick = thick

th + in = thin

th + ud = thud

th + ug = thug

Th**ud**! The **thug** hit the log.

콩! 그 폭력배가 통나무를 쳤어.

Is the glass **thin** or **thick**?

그 유리가 얇아 아니면 두꺼워?

I guess the stems are **thick** enough.

그 정도면 줄기 굵기가 충분한 것 같네.

059

th- ②

than / **th**at / **th**em / **th**is

th + an = than

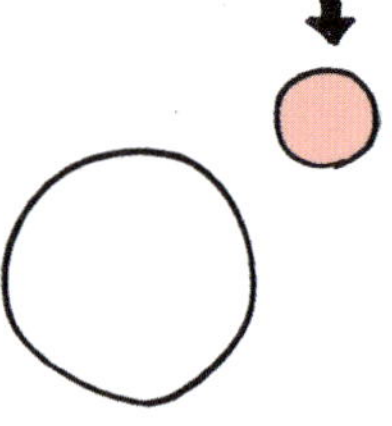

th + at = that

th + em = them

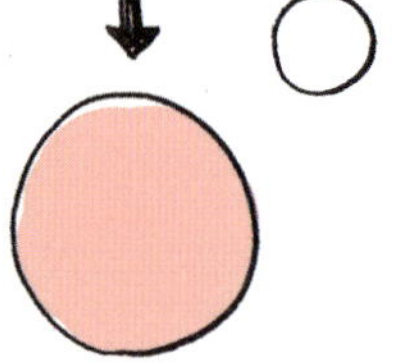

th + is = this

This is big and **th**at is not.
이건 크고 저건 안 커.

Mine is less **th**an yours.
내 것이 네 것보다 적어.

This snack is for **th**em.
이 간식은 그들을 위한 거야.

060

kn-

knack / **kn**it / **kn**ob /
knock / **kn**ot

kn + ack = knack

kn + it = knit

kn + ob = knob

kn + ock = knock

kn + ot = knot

Knock! **Kn**ock!
– Find the **kn**ob and come in!

똑똑! – 문 손잡이 찾아서 들어와!

Now I can **kn**it!
– Yes, I see you got the **kn**ack.

나 이제 뜨개질 할 수 있어! – 그래, 이제야 감 잡은 것 같네.

How can I get rid of a **kn**ot when I **kn**it?

뜨개질 할 때 매듭은 어떻게 없애지?

061

wr-

wrap / **wr**ath / **wr**eck /
wren / **wr**ist

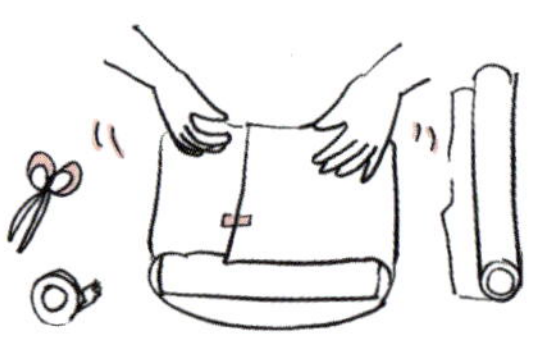

wr + ap = wrap

wr + ath = wrath

wr + eck = wreck

wr + en = wren

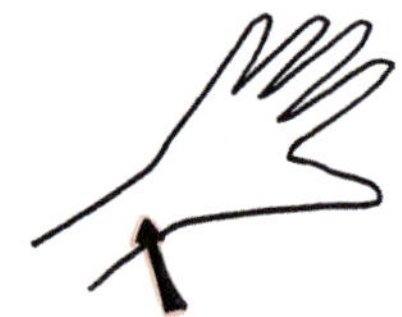

wr + ist = wrist

Wrap your **wr**ist with this.

이걸로 손목을 감싸.

Do you see the **wren** on the **wreck**?

저기 난파선 위에 굴뚝새 보여?

The **wrath** of God came upon them.

신의 분노가 그들에게 내렸다.

062

qu-

quack / **qu**ick / **qu**ill / **qu**ilt / **qu**it / **qu**iz

qu + ack = quack

qu + ick = quick

qu + ill = quill

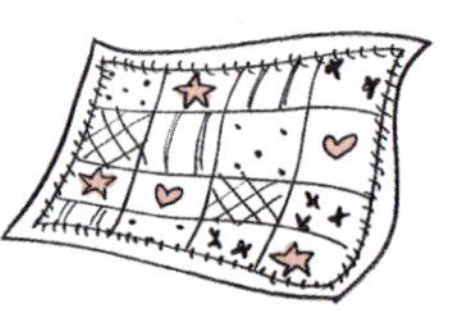

qu + ilt = quilt

qu + it = quit

qu + iz = quiz

He was **quick** to **quit**.

그 사람 빨리도 그만두더라.

Quack! **Quack**! The ducks are under the **quilt**.

꽥꽥! 조각보 아래에 오리들이 있어.

Use this **quill** when you take the **quiz**.

시험 칠 때 이 깃펜을 써.

063

-(t)ch

rich / **mu**ch / **ca**tch / **fe**tch /
hatch / **pa**tch

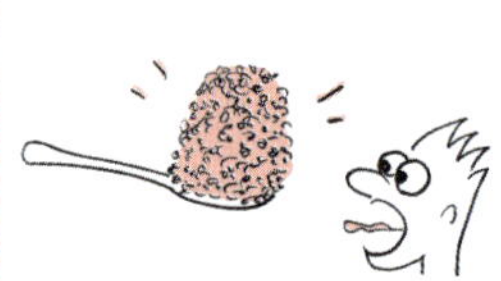

r + i**ch** = rich   m + u**ch** = much   c + a**tch** = catch

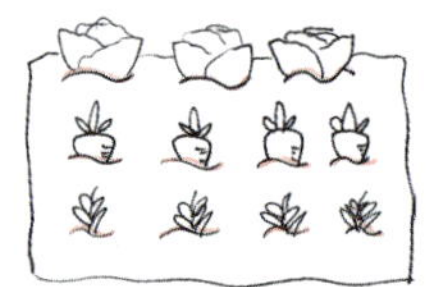

f + e**tch** = fetch   h + a**tch** = hatch   p + a**tch** = patch

I'm **rich** and I love that very **much**.

난 부자야. 내가 부자라는 게 너무 좋아.

Catch me if you can!
– Go **fetch** him!

나 잡아 봐라! – 가서 저 녀석을 잡아와.

Did you see the chick **hatch** on the **patch**?

그 텃밭에서 병아리가 부화하는 거 봤어?

064

-sh

flash / crash / fresh / dish / fish / wish / rush / blush / crush

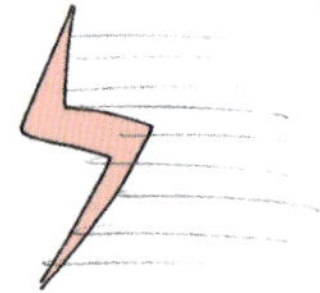

fl + a**sh** = flash

cr + a**sh** = crash

fr + e**sh** = fresh

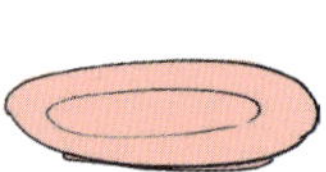

d + i**sh** = dish

f + i**sh** = fish

w + i**sh** = wish

r + u**sh** = rush

bl + u**sh** = blush

cr + u**sh** = crush

A **fre**sh **fi**sh on a **di**sh! Like I always **wi**sh!

접시에 놓인 신선한 물고기라! 내가 항상 바라는 거야!

There was a **cra**sh in a **fla**sh.
- Did you **ru**sh to see it?

눈 깜짝할 사이에 충돌이 일어났어. – 달려가서 봤어?

I saw you **blu**sh when you said you had a **cru**sh on him.

네가 그를 짝사랑 한다고 말할 때 네 얼굴이 붉어지는 걸 봤어.

065

-th

bath** / **ma**th** / **mo**th** /
sloth** / **bro**th**

b + a**th** = bath

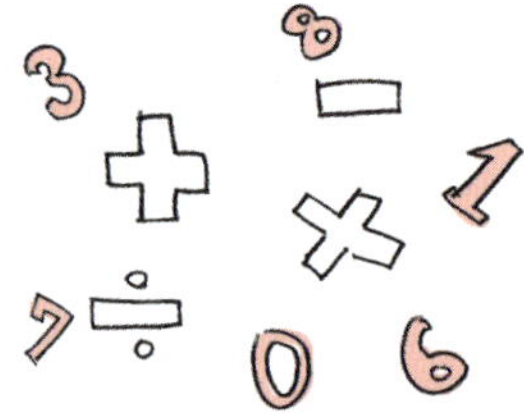

m + a**th** = math

m + o**th** = moth

sl + o**th** = sloth

br + o**th** = broth

Both of you need a **bath**.

너희 둘 다 목욕해야 해.

Can the **sloth** also do **math**? Seriously?

그 나무늘보도 수학을 할 줄 안다고? 진짜?

There's a **moth** in the **broth**! Yuck!

수프에 나방이 있어! 으웩!

066

-ng

fang / **ga**ng / **ki**ng / **ri**ng /
sing / **wi**ng / **swi**ng / **lo**ng

f + a**ng** = fang

g + a**ng** = gang

k + i**ng** = king

r + i**ng** = ring

s + i**ng** = sing

w + i**ng** = wing

sw + i**ng** = swing

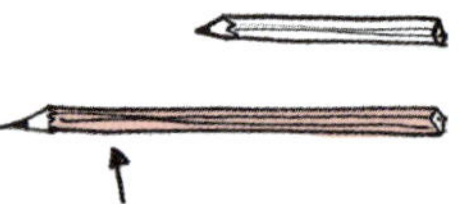

l + o**ng** = long

She likes to **sing** on a **swing**.

그녀는 그네를 타며 노래하는 걸 좋아한다.

It's got **long fang**s and large **wing**s!

그건 긴 송곳니와 커다란 날개를 갖고 있어!

The **king** has a **ring** and the **gang** wants it.

왕이 반지를 하나 갖고 있는데 그 조직이 그걸 노려.

067

-ing

jogging / singing / swimming / grinning / knitting

jog + g + **ing** = jogging

sing + **ing** = singing

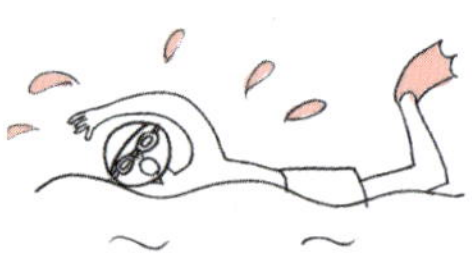

swim + m + **ing** = swimming

grin + n + **ing** = grinning

knit + t + **ing** = knitting

Why is he **grinning** at me?

저 사람은 왜 나를 보고 웃고 있는 거야?

I saw her **singing** as she was **knitting**.

나는 그녀가 뜨개질을 하며 노래 부르는 걸 보았다.

Which do you like better, **jogging** or **swimming**?

조깅이랑 수영 중에 뭐가 더 좋아?

068

-sk

ask / **ba**sk / **ma**sk / **ta**sk /
whisk / **du**sk / **ru**sk

ask

b + a**sk** = bask

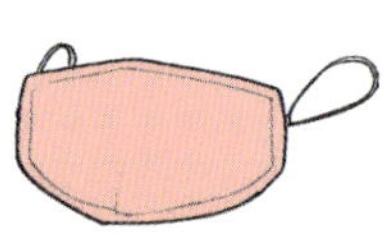

m + a**sk** = mask

t + a**sk** = task

wh + i**sk** = whisk

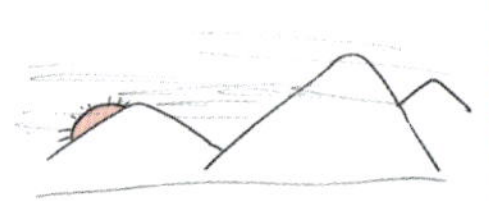

d + u**sk** = dusk

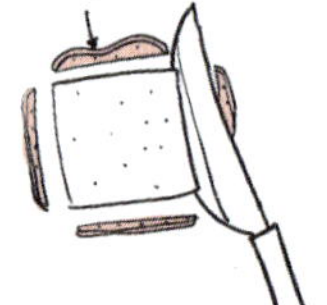

r + u**sk** = rusk

Ask him if he wants to **ba**sk in the sun.

햇볕 쬐러 나가고 싶은지 그에게 물어봐.

Our **ta**sk is to get the **ma**sk before **du**sk.

해지기 전에 가면을 손에 넣는 게 우리의 임무야.

You need a **whi**sk to make **ru**sks.

과자를 만들려면 거품기가 필요해.

069

-st

fast / **la**st / **be**st / **ne**st /
test / **mi**st / **lo**st

f + a**st** = fast

l + a**st** = last

b + e**st** = best

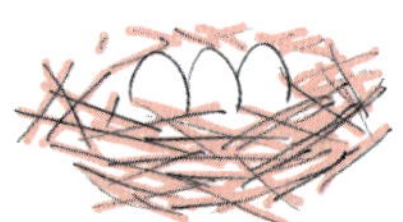

n + e**st** = nest

t + e**st** = test

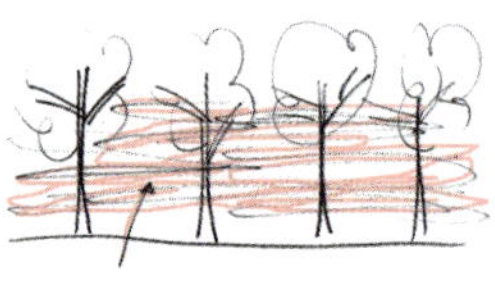

m + i**st** = mist

l + o**st** = lost

She took the **test** and she was the **best**.

그녀는 시험을 치렀고 최고의 성적을 받았다.

He wasn't **fast** enough and came in **last**.

그는 그렇게 빠르지 않았고 꼴찌로 들어왔다.

I got **lost** in the **mist** as I was looking for the **nest**.

둥지를 찾다가 안개 속에 길을 잃었어.

070

-ft

raft / **gi**ft / **si**ft / **dri**ft /
swift / **the**ft / **so**ft

r + a**ft** = raft

g + i**ft** = gift

s + i**ft** = sift

dr + i**ft** = drift

sw + i**ft** = swift

th + e**ft** = theft

s + o**ft** = soft

That **si**ft is too **so**ft, isn't it?
그 체는 너무 물렁물렁해, 그렇지?

That's **the**ft, not a **gi**ft.
그건 선물이 아니고 절도야.

Drift along on a **swi**ft ra**ft**.
빠른 뗏목을 타고 물살을 따라가.

071

-mp

camp / **cha**mp / **bli**mp /
bump / **ju**mp / **stu**mp

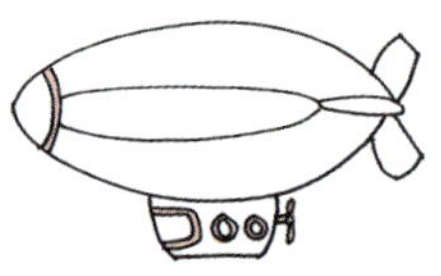

c + a**mp** = camp

ch + a**mp** = champ

bl + i**mp** = blimp

b + u**mp** = bump

j + u**mp** = jump

st + u**mp** = stump

Let's **camp** there near the **stump**.

저기 나무 그루터기 근처에서 야영하자.

Why does the **champ** have a **bump**?

저 챔피언은 왜 혹이 났지?

What? He will **jump** off the **blimp**?

뭐? 그가 비행선에서 뛰어내릴 거라고?

072

-lk

bulk / hulk / milk / sulk / silk

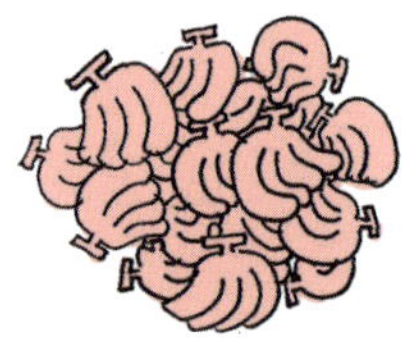

b + u**lk** = bulk

h + u**lk** = hulk

m + i**lk** = milk

s + u**lk** = sulk

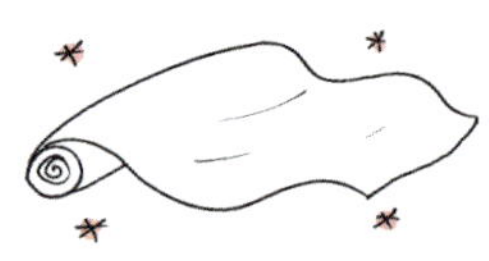

s + i**lk** = silk

Hulk doesn't **sulk**. He just gets mad.

헐크는 삐치지 않아. 화를 낼 뿐이지.

I got some **milk** on my **silk** dress.

내 실크 드레스에 우유가 묻었어.

Those quills only come in **bulk**.

저 깃펜들은 묶음으로만 나와.

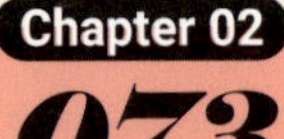

073

-lp

alp / he**lp** / pu**lp** /
gu**lp** / sca**lp**

a**lp**

h + e**lp** = help

p + u**lp** = pulp

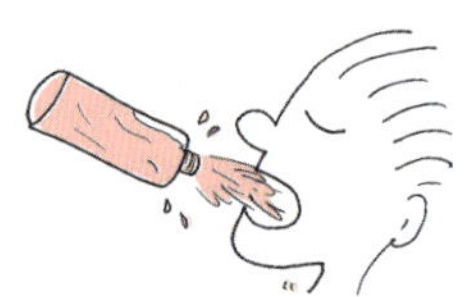

g + u**lp** = gulp

sc + a**lp** = scalp

Gulp it with the **pulp**.

그거 과육이랑 같이 마셔.

Have you been to the **Alp**s?

알프스산맥에 가본 적 있니?

Can you **help** me with my **scalp**?

내 두피 문제 해결하는 것 좀 도와줄래?

074

-lt

bel**t** / **me**l**t** / **kne**l**t** / **ki**l**t** /
wil**t** / **insu**l**t**

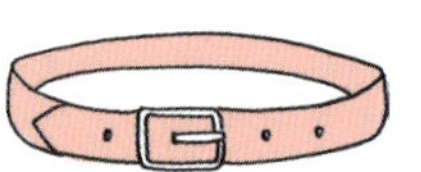

b + e**lt** = belt

m + e**lt** = melt

kn + e**lt** = knelt

k + i**lt** = kilt

w + i**lt** = wilt

in·s + u**lt** = insult

It won't **melt** or **wilt**.

그건 녹거나 시들지 않을거야.

You need a **belt** on the **kilt** to fix it.

킬트를 고정하려면 벨트를 매야 해.

I **knelt**. That was quite **insult**ing.

난 무릎을 꿇었어. 정말 굴욕적이었지.

075

-nd

hand / **sa**nd / **be**nd / **me**nd /
lend / **se**nd / **spe**nd

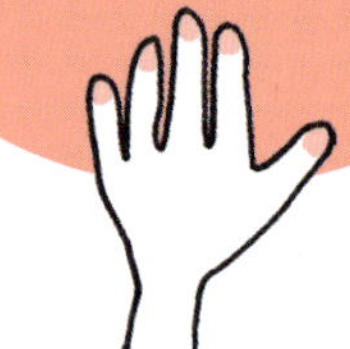

h + a**nd** = hand

s + a**nd** = sand

b + e**nd** = bend

m + e**nd** = mend

l + e**nd** = lend

s + e**nd** = send

sp + e**nd** = spend

Bend and put your **hand**s in the **sand**.

몸을 굽혀 모래 속에 손을 넣어 봐.

Can you **mend** it and **send** it back to me?

그거 수리해서 저한테 다시 보내주실 수 있나요?

I can't **spend** any more time on this. Let's just **lend** it to them.

더는 여기에 시간을 쓸 수 없어. 그거 그냥 저들에게 빌려 줘.

076

-nt

ant / **pla**nt / **cha**nt / **te**nt / **pri**nt / **hu**nt

a**nt**

pl + a**nt** = plant

ch + a**nt** = chant

t + e**nt** = tent

pr + i**nt** = print

h + u**nt** = hunt

The **pla**n**t**s got many **a**n**t**s.

그 식물들에는 개미가 많아.

We will put up a **te**n**t** and then go **hu**n**t**ing.

우린 텐트를 치고 나서 사냥을 갈 거야.

Pri**nt** it out so that we can all **cha**n**t** together.

우리 모두가 함께 부를 수 있게 그것 좀 출력해.

077

-nk

thank / **pi**nk / **wi**nk / **sti**nk /
drink / **thi**nk / **sku**nk

th + ank = tha**nk**

p + ink = pi**nk**

w + ink = wi**nk**

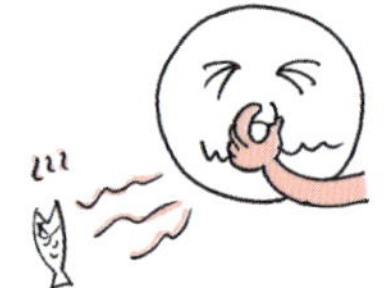

st + ink = sti**nk**

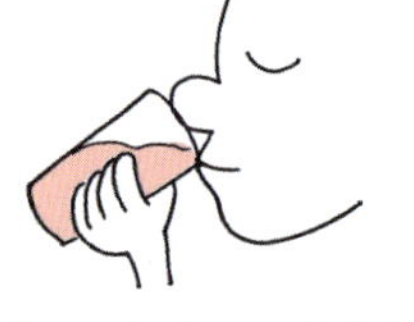

dr + ink = dri**nk**

th + ink = thi**nk**

sk + unk = sku**nk**

Oh! The **skunk stink**s!

으앗! 스컹크 냄새가 너무 지독해!

Thank you for the **pink drink**.

분홍색 음료 주셔서 감사해요.

I **think** about your **wink** every day.

난 매일 네 윙크 생각해.

Chapter 3

'끝까지' 잘 발음하자!

복수형 -es, 동사의 과거형 -ed 등
다양한 끝소리를 정확하게 발음할 수 있어요.

UNIT
078~083

078

-ly

ugly / **bel**ly / **glad**ly /
smelly / **soft**ly / **quick**ly

ugly

belly

gladly

smelly

softly

quickly

That thing is **ugly** and **smelly**.
그건 못 생기고 냄새도 나.

Come **quickly**, will you?
– **Gladly**!
어서 와, 응? – 네!

Rub your **belly softly**.
배를 살살 문질러.

079

-le

little / **bott**le / **cudd**le / **ratt**le / **hand**le / **midd**le / **gigg**le

litt**le**

bott**le**

cudd**le**

ratt**le**

hand**le**

midd**le**

gigg**le**

Grab the **middle** of the **handle**.

손잡이 중간을 잡아.

I want to **cuddle** her and give her a **bottle**.

그 아가를 안고 우유 먹이고 싶어.

The **little** kid **giggle**s when he plays with his **rattle**.

그 꼬마는 딸랑이를 갖고 놀 때 킥킥대.

080

-es

axes** / box**es** / branch**es** /
dish**es** / glass**es** / match**es**

ax**es**

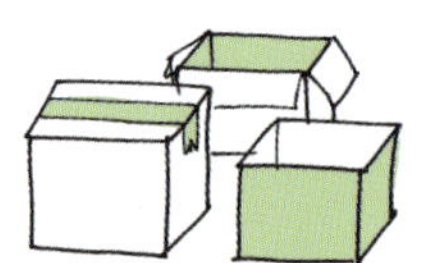

box**es**

branch**es**

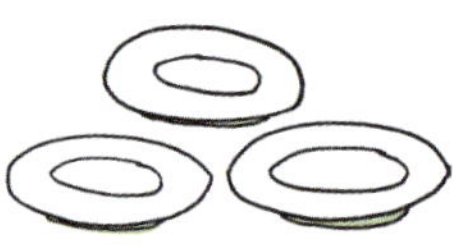

dish**es**

glass**es**

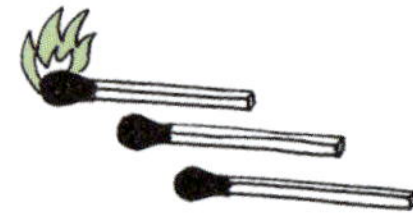

match**es**

Why do you need **ax****es**, not **box****es**?

넌 왜 상자가 아니라 도끼가 필요해?

He made **match****es** out of **branch****es**.

그는 나뭇가지로 성냥을 만들었다.

Would you put these **dish****es** and **glass****es** back?

이 접시들이랑 유리잔들 좀 도로 갖다 놔 줄래?

081

-ed ①

added / **blended** / **lifted** / **mended** / **rested** / **tilted** / **chanted**

add**ed**

blend**ed**

lift**ed**

mend**ed**

rest**ed**

tilt**ed**

chant**ed**

They all **rested** after they **chanted**.

그들은 함께 노래한 후 모두 휴식을 취했다.

Dad **lifted** the **tilted** swings and **mended** them.

아빠는 기울어진 그네들을 들어 올려 수리했다.

Mom **added** an egg and **blended** it with some milk.

엄마는 달걀 하나를 넣어 우유와 섞었다.

082

-ed [2]

rubbed / **wagged** / **sobbed** /
hugged / **filled**

rubbed

wagged

sobbed

hugged

filled

The dog **wagged** and **rubbed** the dish.

그 개는 꼬리 치며 접시를 문질렀다.

They **hugged** each other and **sobbed**.

그들은 서로를 끌어안고 흐느꼈다.

The man **filled** it with jam.

그 남자는 거기에 잼을 채워 넣었다.

083

-ed [3]

packed / **sipp**ed / **lick**ed / **pick**ed / **shock**ed / **chopp**ed

pack**ed**

sipp**ed**

lick**ed**

pick**ed**

shock**ed**

chopp**ed**

The cat **lick**ed and **lick**ed the **chopp**ed fish.

그 고양이는 잘게 썬 생선을 핥고 또 핥았다.

I **pick**ed up the cup and **sipp**ed some water from it.

난 컵을 들어 안에 있는 물을 조금 마셨어.

She was so **shock**ed that he'd **pack**ed up and just left.

그녀는 그가 짐을 싸서 그냥 떠나버렸다는 사실에 엄청난 충격을 받았다.

Chapter 4

모음의 새시대, 장모음, 이중모음 & more!

각 모음이 자기 이름대로 소리 나는 장모음과
이중모음 및 다양한 모음의 변주를 맛 보아요.

084

a_e

safe / **bake** / **cake** / **snake** /
chase / **hate** / **skate** / **cave**

s**afe**

b**ake**

c**ake**

sn**ake**

ch**ase**

h**ate**

sk**ate**

c**ave**

Is it **safe** to **skate** around the **cave**?

동굴 주변에서 스케이트 타는 게 안전할까?

I saw them **chase snake**s.

그 애들이 뱀을 쫓아가는 걸 봤어요.

I **hate** to **bake** the same **cake** every day!

매일 똑같은 케이크 굽는 게 너무 싫어!

085

ai

fail / rain / sail / wait / snail / train / paint

fail

rain

sail

wait

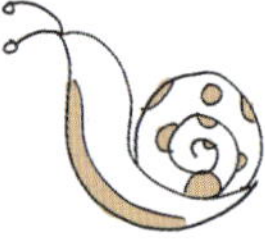

snail

train

paint

Are you **wait**ing for the **train**?

기차 기다리세요?

The **snail fail**ed to go through the **rain**.

그 달팽이는 비를 뚫고 가지 못했다.

Paint the word on the **sail**.

돛에다 그 말을 써넣어.

086

ay

day / pay / say / way / stay / clay / play

day

pay

say

way

stay

clay

play

There's no **way** I would **pay** for this.

난 이 돈 절대 안 낼 거야.

They **play** with **clay** every **day**.

걔들은 매일 점토 갖고 놀아.

She's **say**ing that she's going to **stay**.

그녀는 여기에 남겠다는 거야.

087

ey ①

hey / g**r**ey / **wh**ey / **th**ey

hey

grey

wh**ey**

th**ey**

Hey! Why is that thing **grey**?

어이! 그건 왜 회색이야?

Are **they** going to drink that **wh**ey?

그들이 그 유청을 마실 거라고?

They never say **hey** or hi to me.

그들은 절대 나에게 말을 걸거나 인사하지 않아.

088

eigh

neigh / weigh / sleigh / eight / weight / freight

neigh

weigh

sleigh

eight

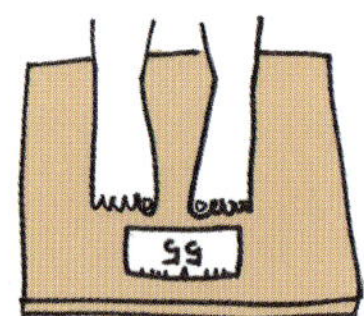

weigh**t**

freigh**t**

The **freight** train must **weigh** a lot.

그 화물열차는 무게가 엄청 나갈 거야.

That thing on the **sleigh** said, "**Neigh**!"

썰매에 달린 그게 "히이잉" 소리를 냈어.

It's been **eight** years since I last saw her.
She's put on some **weight**.

마지막으로 그녀를 본 지 8년이 되었어. 그동안 살이 좀 쪘네.

089

i_e

**ride / knife / bike / hike /
like / lime / wine / white**

ride

knife

bike

hike

like

lime

wine

white

We need a **knife** to cut the **lime**.
라임을 자르려면 우린 칼이 필요해.

I think the **white wine** tastes fine!
나는 그 화이트와인 맛 괜찮은 것 같은데!

Do you **like hik**ing or **rid**ing a **bike**?
하이킹 하는 걸 좋아하세요 아니면 자전거 타는 걸 좋아하세요?

090

-ie① & -ye

lie / **pie** / **tie** /
bye / **rye** / **dye**

lie

pie

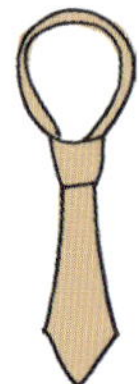

tie

bye

rye

dye

You **lie** and we say, "**Bye-bye**." OK?

너 거짓말하면 우리랑은 끝이야. 알겠어?

My friend made a **pie** with a **rye** crust. Yum!

내 친구가 윗부분을 호밀로 덮은 파이를 만들었는데 맛있어.

You **dye**d these **tie**s yourself? How?

네가 이 넥타이들을 직접 염색했다고? 어떻게?

091

igh

sigh / th**igh** / n**igh**t / f**igh**t / l**igh**t / r**igh**t / t**igh**t / s**igh**t

sigh

th**igh**

n**igh**t

f**igh**t

l**igh**t

r**igh**t

t**igh**t

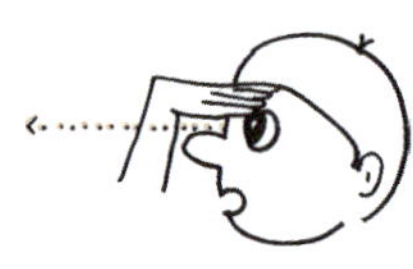

s**igh**t

The **fight** went on all **night** long. **S**i**gh**!

다툼은 밤새 계속되었어. 휴!

You're **right**. Out of **sight**, out of mind.

네 말이 맞아. 눈에서 멀어지면 마음에서도 멀어져.

Those are too **light** and too **tight** in the **thigh**s!

그건 너무 얇고 허벅지에 꽉 끼잖아!

092

ind

bind / **f**ind / **k**ind / **m**ind /
blind / **gr**ind

bind

find

kind

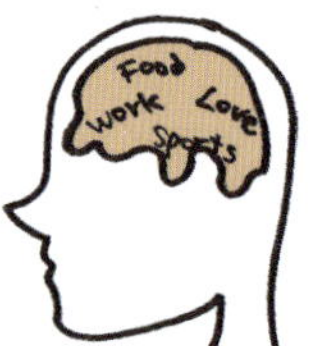

mind

blind

grind

The **bl**ind woman wants to **f**ind her home.

앞을 보지 못하는 그 여인은 자신의 집을 찾고 싶어해.

It's so **k**ind of you to **b**ind them for me!

절 위해 그것들을 묶어 주시다니 정말 친절하시네요!

Are you out of your **m**ind?
Why did you **gr**ind it all?

너 정신 나갔어? 그걸 왜 다 갈았어?

093

o_e

**hole / home / hope / note /
broke / smoke / stove /
wrote**

hole

home

hope

note

broke

smoke

stove

wrote

There is **smoke** coming from that **hole**!

저 구멍에서 연기가 나고 있어!

I **wrote** a **note** that said, "I **broke** your **stove**."

내가 네 가스렌지를 망가뜨렸다고 쪽지 썼었는데.

Don't get your **hope**s up. He may not come **home**.

너무 기대하진 마. 그는 집으로 안 올지도 몰라.

094

oe&-o

doe / toe /
go / no / yoyo / banjo

doe

toe

go

no

yoyo

banjo

Go out and play with the **yoyo**.

나가서 요요 갖고 놀아.

No, I can't play the **banjo**.

아뇨, 저 밴조 연주할 줄 몰라요.

She painted another **doe** on her **toe** nail.

그녀는 발톱에 암사슴을 한 마리 더 그려 넣었다.

095

oa

**boat / coat / moat / goat /
float / toad / foam / soap**

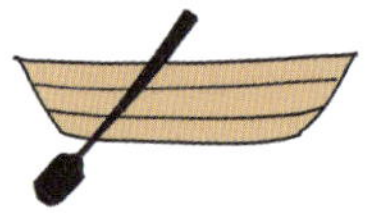

boat

coat

moat

goat

float

toad

foam

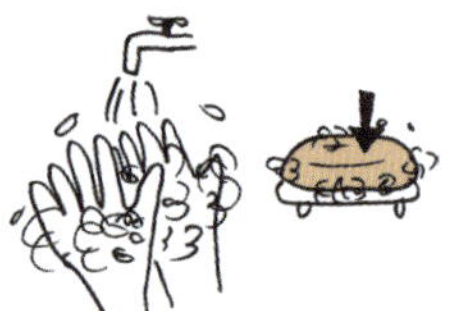

soap

That **soap** makes a lot of **foam**.

그 비누는 거품이 많이 나.

Look! **Boat**s are **float**ing in the **moat**!

저길 봐! 해자에 배들이 떠다니고 있어!

What's that under your **coat**? A **goat**?
– No, it's a **toad**!

네 코트 속에 그건 뭐야? 염소? – 아니, 두꺼비야!

096

OW ①

bow / sh**ow** / sl**ow** / sn**ow** /
blow / fl**ow** / gl**ow** / gr**ow**

bow

sh**ow**

sl**ow**

sn**ow**

blow

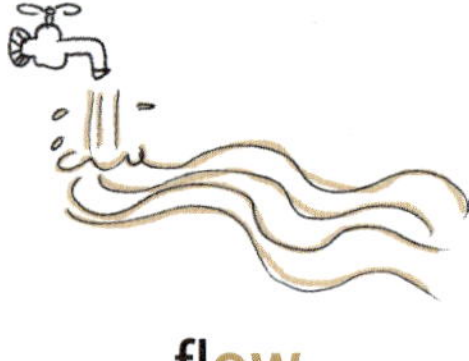

fl**ow**

gl**ow**

gr**ow**

The wind **blow**s and the water **flow**s.
바람이 불고 물이 흐른다.

Let me **show** you how the **bow glow**s
in the **snow**.
그 리본이 어떻게 눈 속에서 빛나는지 보여줄게.

They are known to **grow** rather **slow**ly.
그것들은 좀 천천히 자란다고 알려져 있다.

097

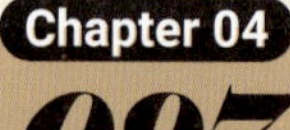

old

old / **c**old / **f**old / **g**old /
hold / **m**old / **s**old / **sc**old

old

cold

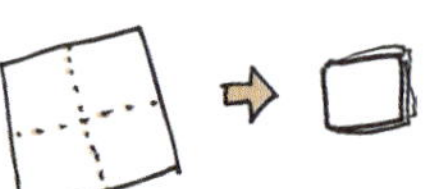

fold

gold

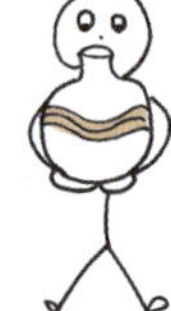

hold

mold

sold

scold

The **old mold** was **sold** a long time ago.

그 낡은 틀은 오래전에 팔렸어요.

Their father **scold**ed them for **hold**ing the **gold** bottle wrong.

그들의 아버지는 황금 병을 잘못 들고 있다고 그들을 꾸짖었다.

Un**fold** this cape and put it on when you're **cold**.

추울 때 이 망토를 펴서 둘러.

098

e_e & _e

eve / **theme** /
be / **he** / **me** / **we** / **she**

eve

theme

be

he

me

we

she

We should not **be** late. Don't you think so?

우리 늦으면 안 돼. 너도 그렇게 생각하지 않아?

He asked **me** out on Christmas **Eve**!

그가 크리스마스이브에 데이트 신청했어!

She must **be** the one who decides on the **theme**.

그녀가 주제에 대한 결정권자임이 틀림없어.

099

ee

fee**l** / **m**ee**t** / **f**r**ee** / **tr**ee** /
shee**p** / **wh**ee**l** / **kn**ee**l** /
quee**n**

f**ee**l

m**ee**t

fr**ee**

tr**ee**

sh**ee**p

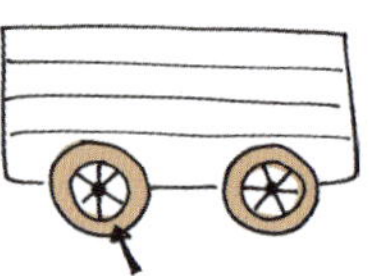

wh**ee**l

kn**ee**l

qu**ee**n

"**Kn**eel!" said the **qu**e**en** as she saw the man on **wh**ee**l**s.

"무릎을 꿇어라!" 여왕은 자전거 탄 남자를 보자 말했다.

There might be some **sh**ee**p** under the **tr**ee.

나무 아래에 양이 몇 마리 있을지도 몰라요.

Feel free to come **m**ee**t** me any time!

언제든 나 만나러 와!

100

ea

**pea / sea / bean / eat / meat
/ beach / peach / reach**

p**ea**

sea

b**ea**n

eat

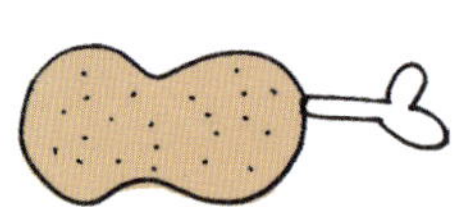

m**ea**t

b**ea**ch

p**ea**ch

r**ea**ch

I like to **eat pea**s and **bean**s with **meat**.

난 여러 가지 콩을 고기와 함께 먹는 걸 좋아해.

A **beach** is a land beside the **sea**.

해변은 바다 옆에 있는 땅이야.

Reach for the best **peach** in the tree.

나무에 달린 가장 맛있는 복숭아로 손을 뻗어 봐.

101

_ey ②

**key / hockey / alley /
chimney / valley / trolley**

key

hockey

alley

chimney

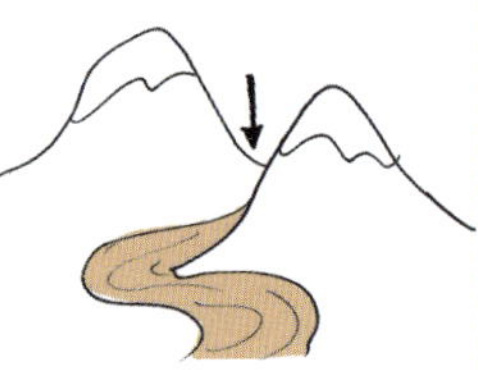

valley

trolley

Don't play **hockey** near the **valley**.

계곡 근처에서 하키 하지 마.

The **trolley** is too big to go through the **alley**.

골목을 지나가기엔 카트가 너무 커.

You'll have to go down the **chimney** if you don't have the **key**.

열쇠가 없으면 굴뚝을 타고 아래로 내려가야 할걸.

102

ie ②

th<u>ie</u>f / **y<u>ie</u>ld** / **ch<u>ie</u>f** /
zomb<u>ie</u> / **hood<u>ie</u>** / **self<u>ie</u>**

th**ie**f

y**ie**ld

ch**ie**f

zomb**ie**

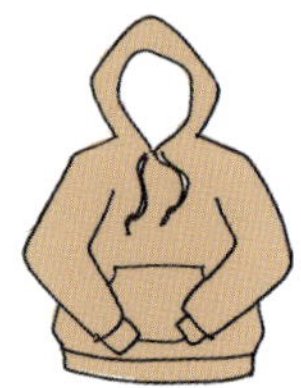

hood**ie**

self**ie**

They've never seen their **chief yield**.

그들은 추장이 굴복하는 것을 한 번도 본 적이 없다.

I like your **selfie** in the pink **hoodie**.

너 핑크색 후드티 입고 찍은 셀카 좋더라.

Fight the **zombie** or the **thief**.

좀비랑 싸우든지 도둑이랑 싸우든지.

103

u_e ①

puke / tune / fuse /
muse / cute / mute

puke

tune

fuse

muse

cute

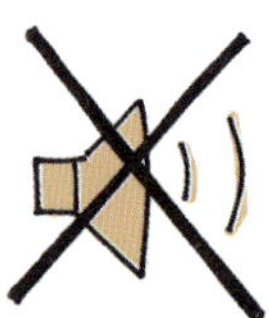

mute

His **muse** helped him come up with the **tune**s.

그의 뮤즈는 그가 곡을 만드는 것을 도왔다.

Well, she was **cute** before she **puke**d on me.

그게, 그녀가 나에게 토하기 전까지는 귀여웠지.

Everything went **mute** when he cut the **fuse**.

그가 퓨즈를 자르자 모든 것이 조용해졌다.

104

u_e ②

dude / **rude** / **rule** / **lute** /
flute / **jukebox**

dude

rude

rule

lute

flute

jukebox

Don't be so **rude**. We've got some **rule**s here.

그렇게 무례하게 굴지마. 이곳에는 규칙이 있어.

Dude, where did you get that **jukebox**?

야, 그 주크박스 어디서 났어?

Which one do you want, the **lute** or the **flute**?

류트랑 플루트 중에 뭐 할래?

105

ue & ui

**blue / clue / glue /
true / suit / fruit**

blue

clue

glue

true

suit

fruit

That's **true**. I don't have any **clue**s.

맞아. 나 하나도 모르겠어.

The **blue suit** looks great on you.

그 파란 정장 너한테 잘 어울린다.

I'm going shopping for some **fruit** and **glue**.

과일이랑 풀 좀 사러 가는 길이야.

106

ew

chew / flew / blew / threw / drew / new

chew

flew

blew

threw

drew

new

The **new** kid was **chew**ing gum.

새로 온 아이는 껌을 씹고 있었다.

He **drew** something and **threw** it to me.

그는 뭔가를 그려 내게로 던졌다.

The wind **blew** and my cape **flew** away.

바람이 불어서 내 망토가 날아갔어.

107

OO [1]

**moon / pool / roof / room /
zoo / igloo / broom**

moon

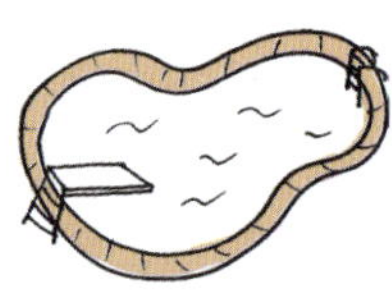

pool

roof

room

zoo

igloo

broom

Get the **broom** and clean your **room**!

빗자루 가져와서 네 방 청소해!

We sat on the **roof** and watched the **moon** together.

우리는 지붕에 앉아 함께 달을 바라보았다.

They built an **igloo** and a **pool** at the **zoo**.

그들은 동물원에 이글루와 수영장을 만들었다.

108

oo ②

book / **c**ook / **h**ood /
hook / **l**ook / **w**ood

book

cook

hood

hook

look

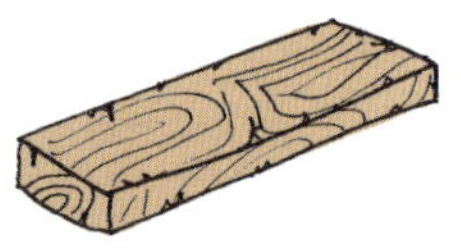

wood

Those **hook**s are made of **wood**.

그 고리들은 나무로 만들었어.

You **look** like your brother with your **hood** on.

너 모자 쓰니까 네 형 닮았어.

I got this **book** from the **cook**.

나 이 책 그 요리사한테서 받은 거야.

109

oi

oi / b**oi**l / f**oi**l / j**oi**n /
m**oi**st / p**oi**nt / s**oi**l

oi

b**oi**l

f**oi**l

j**oi**n

m**oi**st

p**oi**nt

s**oi**l

The **soil** seems **moist** enough.

흙은 충분히 촉촉한 것 같아.

Wrap it well with **foil** and cook it in the **boil**ing **oil**.

그거 포일로 잘 싸서 끓는 기름에다 넣어 익혀.

"**Join** us!" he said as he **point**ed at me.

"같이 하자!" 그는 나를 가리키며 말했다.

110

oy

boy / **j**oy / **s**oy /
toy / **cl**oy / **Tr**oy

boy

joy

soy

toy

cloy

Troy

Boy**s** love to play with **to**y**s** that move.

남자아이들은 움직이는 장난감을 가지고 노는 걸 좋아한다.

They jumped for **joy** at the news about **Troy**.

그들은 트로이 소식에 기뻐 날뛰었다.

The **soy** milk has really begun to **cloy**.

그 두유 정말로 물리기 시작했어.

ou

outcast / couch / loud /
mouth / pout / round /
proud / shout

outcast

couch

l**ou**d

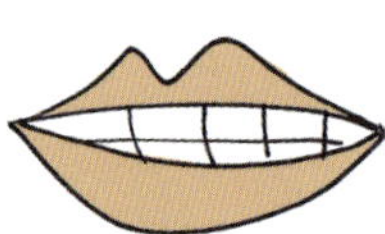

m**ou**th

p**ou**t

r**ou**nd

pr**ou**d

sh**ou**t

Open your **mouth** and **shout** out **loud**!

입을 벌리고 크게 소리 질러!

His mom is **proud** of his grades even though he's an **outcast**.

그가 왕따인데도 그의 엄마는 아들의 성적만 자랑스러워한다.

Stop **pout**ing about the **round couch**.

둥근 소파 때문에 뿌루퉁해 있는 거 그만해.

OW ②

bow / cow / scowl / clown / brown / crowd / crown / frown

b**ow**

c**ow**

sc**ow**l

cl**ow**n

br**ow**n

cr**ow**d

cr**ow**n

fr**ow**n

They **bow**ed down to the **clown** with a **crown**.

그들은 왕관을 쓴 광대에게 절했다.

The **crowd frown**ed and **scowl**ed at him.

사람들은 눈살을 찌푸리며 그를 노려보았다.

We heard the sound of the **brown cow**.

우리는 그 갈색 소의 소리를 들었다.

113

au

daunt / fault / haunt / vault / flaunt / fraud

daunt

fault

haunt

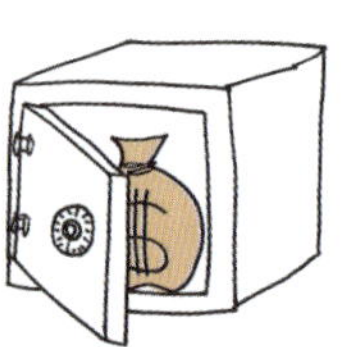

vault

flaunt

fraud

It's not my **fault** we ended up in the **haunt**ed house!

우리가 귀신의 집까지 오게 된 건 내 잘못이 아니야!

He felt **daunt**ed when his friends **flaunt**ed how rich they were.

그는 친구들이 자신이 얼마나 부자인지 자랑할 때 기가 죽었다.

They got themselves a big **vault** full of gold by **fraud**.

그들은 사기로 금이 가득 든 금고를 손에 넣었다.

114

aw

**hawk / jaw / lawn / paw /
draw / yawn / claw / crawl**

hawk

jaw

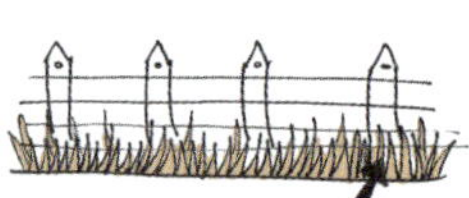

lawn

paw

draw

yawn

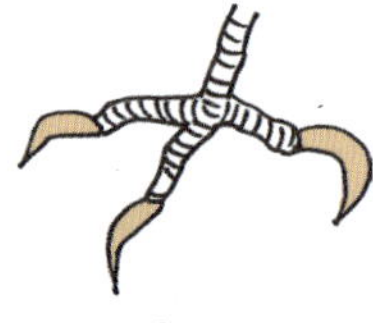

claw

crawl

Now **draw** the **claw**s of the **hawk** family.

이제 매 가족의 발톱을 그리세요.

When you **yawn**, your **jaw**s open wide.

하품할 때는 턱이 크게 벌어진다.

They don't use their **paw**s when they **crawl** on the **lawn**.

그들은 잔디 위를 기어갈 때 발을 사용하지 않는다.

115

all & alk

**ball / call / tall / wall /
small / tall / walk / chalk**

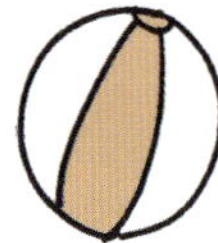

b**all**

c**all**

t**all**

w**all**

sm**all**

t**alk**

w**alk**

ch**alk**

I'll **call** and ask if they sell **ball**s.

내가 전화해서 거기 공 파는지 물어볼게.

Walk along the **tall wall**s.

키 큰 담장을 따라 걸어가.

We kept **talk**ing about the **sm**all **ch**alk.

우리는 그 작은 분필에 대해 계속 얘기했다.

116

ought & aught

bought / **br**ought / **f**ought / **th**ought / **c**aught / **t**aught

bought

brought

fought

thought

caught

taught

I **thought** you'd **bought** the oil. Didn't you?

난 네가 기름 산 줄 알았지. 안 산 거야?

He **caught** a hawk and **brought** it here.

그는 매를 잡아서 이리로 데려왔어.

We **fought** over who'd **taught** the boy to walk.

우리는 누가 그 소년에게 걸음마를 가르쳤는지를 두고 싸웠다.

117

-y ①

**sky / fly / cry /
dry / fry / why**

sky

fly

cry

dry

fry

why

The clouds look like they're **fly**ing in the **sky**!

구름들이 하늘을 날아다니는 것처럼 보여!

Why are you **cry**ing?

너 왜 울고 있어?

Let the cut fruit **dry**. Then **fry** it in the oil.

자른 과일을 말린 다음 기름에 튀기세요.

118

-y ②

happy / sunny / angry / hungry / candy / chubby / lucky / sleepy

happy

sunny

angry

hungry

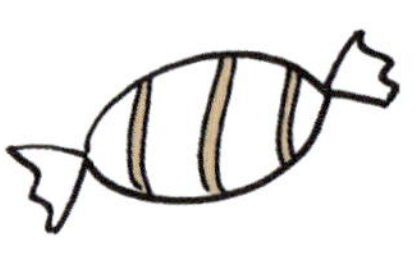

candy

chubby

lucky

sleepy

Why do I get so **sleepy** when it's **sunny**?

나는 날씨가 화창할 때 왜 그렇게 잠이 오지?

The **chubby** boy often gets **angry** when he's **hungry**.

그 통통한 소년은 배 고플 때 종종 화를 난다.

You must be really **happy** to get the **lucky candy**!

행운의 사탕을 얻어서 너 정말 기쁘겠다!

Chapter 5

모음을 조종하는 보스, r!

모음 뒤에 r이 함께 오면 모음의 소리가 바뀌어요.

119

ar

ark / **arm** / **dark** / **far** / **farm** /
shark / **sharp** / **start**

ark

arm

d**ar**k

f**ar**

f**ar**m

sh**ar**k

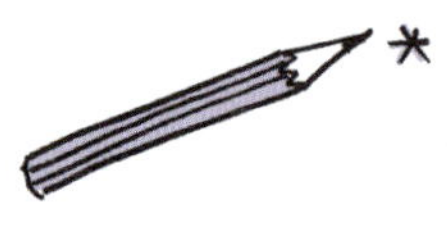

sh**ar**p

st**ar**t

There is a **farm**, but it's **far** from here.

농장이 있긴 한데, 여기서 멀어요.

He **start**ed building an **ark** in the **dark**.

그는 어둠 속에서 방주를 만들기 시작했다.

The **shark** has **sharp** teeth and it can bite your **arm** off.

그 상어는 뾰족한 이빨이 있어서 네 팔을 물어 뜯을수 있어.

120

er

insert / perfect / faster / longer / player / drinker / eater / printer

insert

perfect

faster

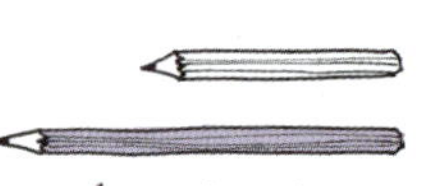

longer

player

drinker

eater

printer

Trains are **faster** than cars. They are **longer**, too!

기차는 차보다 빨라. 더 길기도 하고!

Insert the chip into the **printer**. That's **perfect**!

프린터 안에 칩을 넣어. 완벽해!

That baseball **player** is a big **eater** and a heavy **drinker**.

그 야구선수는 많이 먹고 많이 마신다.

121

ir

bird / birthday / dirty / first / girl / skirt / chirp / shirt

bird

birthday

dirty

first

girl

skirt

chirp

shirt

How do you like your **first birthday** party?

첫 번째 생일파티 마음에 드니?

Take off your **dirty shirt** and **skirt** and put on the new ones.

더러운 셔츠랑 치마 벗고 새 걸로 입어.

The **girl** watched the small **bird chirp**.

소녀는 그 작은 새가 지저귀는 것을 바라보았다.

*1*22

ur

bu**rger** / **b**u**rnt** / **h**u**rt** / **h**u**rry** /
pu**rple** / **s**u**rf** / **t**u**rn** / **yog**u**rt**

bu**rger**

bu**rnt**

hu**rt**

hu**rry**

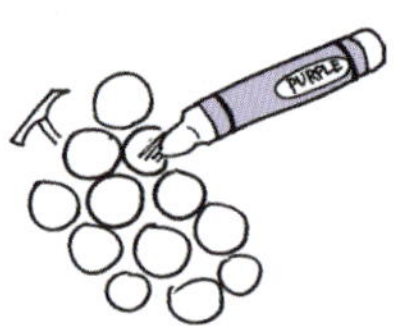

pu**rple**

su**rf**

tu**rn**

yogu**rt**

He got **hurt** while he was **surf**ing.

그는 서핑 하다가 다쳤어.

The **yogurt turn**ed **purple** during the night.

요거트는 밤 사이 보라색으로 변했다.

Dad cooked the **burger** in a **hurry** and **burnt** it.

아빠는 서둘러 버거를 요리하다 태워버렸다.

123

or

**corn / fork / horse / sort /
torch / short / snort / sports**

corn

fork

horse

sort

torch

short

snort

sports

My son ran with a **torch** on **Sports** Day!

내 아들이 운동회에서 횃불을 들고 달렸어요!

Sort the **fork**s into long ones and **short** ones.

포크를 긴 것과 짧은 것으로 나눠.

The **horse snort**ed when the farmer gave him some **corn** to eat.

농부가 옥수수를 먹이로 주자 말은 힝힝거렸다.

124

ore

bored / **m**ore / **st**ore / **sn**ore /
chore / **sh**ore / **ign**ore

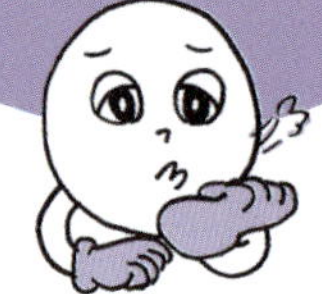

bored

more

store

snore

chore

shore

ignore

There are **more store**s near the **sh**ore.

해안 근처에는 가게들이 더 많아요.

If you're so **bored**, why don't you go and help her with some **chore**s?

그렇게 심심하면 가서 그녀가 집안일 하는 걸 좀 돕지 그래?

He **snore**d so loudly that I couldn't possibly **ignore** it.

그가 코를 너무 크게 골아서 도저히 모른 척할 수가 없었어.

125

our① & our②

cour**t / fo**ur**th / go**ur**d / po**ur** / ho**ur** / so**ur** / flo**ur**

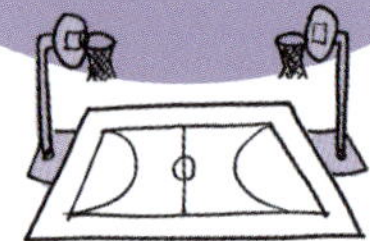

co**ur**t

fo**ur**th

go**ur**d

po**ur**

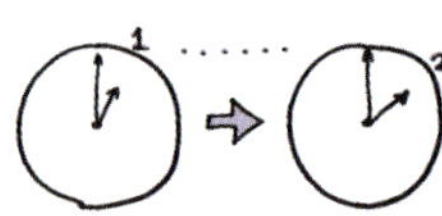

ho**ur**

so**ur**

flo**ur**

The **gourd** has gone bad and it tastes somewhat **sour** now.

박이 상해서 뭔가 시큼한 맛이 나.

Pour the **flour** and water into the bowl. Mix it well and leave it for an **hour**.

밀가루와 물을 큰 그릇에 부어 잘 섞은 후 한 시간 동안 그대로 두세요.

All the **fourth** graders came to the **court**.

4학년 전체가 코트로 나왔다.

126

ear&eer

bear**d** / **f**ear / **h**ear /
near / **t**ear /
deer / **ch**eer

bear**d**

fear

hear

near

tear

deer

cheer

The **deer** was caught by a man with a long **bear**d.

사슴은 긴 턱수염이 있는 남자에게 잡혔다.

Wipe your **tear**s and **cheer** up! We're always here for you.

눈물 닦고 기운 내! 우리는 항상 너와 함께야.

He was so **near** that I could **hear** him saying, "Do not **fear**."

그와 너무 가까운 나머지 그가 "두려워 말아라."하고 말하는 소리를 나는 들을 수 있었다.

127

air & are

fair / pair / chair / stairs / bare / share / scared

fair

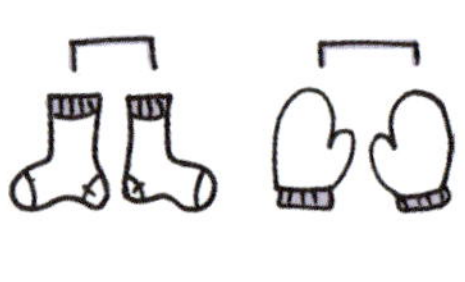

pair

chair

stairs

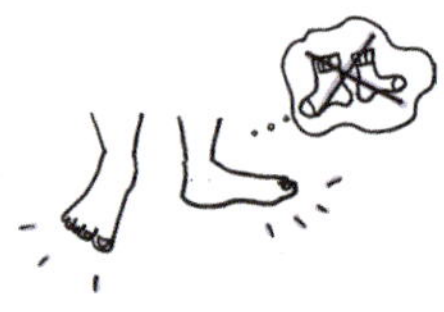

bare

share

scared

That's not **fair**! We all have to **share** the **chair**!

그건 불공평해! 그 의자는 우리 다 같이 써야지!

A **pair** of socks might be good for your **bare** feet.

네 맨발에는 양말 한 켤레가 좋겠구나.

Oh, my God! You **scared** me! I almost fell off the **stairs**!

으악! 너 때문에 놀랐잖아! 나 계단에서 떨어질 뻔했어!

Chapter 6

이것까지 알면
진짜 파닉스 다했다!

알아두면 읽기가 더욱 쉬워지는 추가 패턴들을 알아 봐요.

128

scr & str

**scratch / scrub / scream
strong / string / stress /
stripe**

scratch

scrub

scream

strong

string

stress

stripe

Sometimes, crying and **scream**ing can help blow your **str**ess away.

가끔은 울고 소리 지르는 것이 스트레스를 날려 버리는 데 도움이 될 수 있다.

Add some **str**ings and **stripe**s. Now that's better.

끈이랑 줄무늬를 좀 더해 봐. 훨씬 낫네.

I **scr**atched and **scr**ubbed it, but it wouldn't come off. The glue was too **str**ong.

나는 그것을 긁고 문질렀지만, 풀이 너무 강력해서 그것을 제거할 수 없었다.

129

spr & spl

**spring / sprout /
spray / sprain
split / splint**

spring

sprout

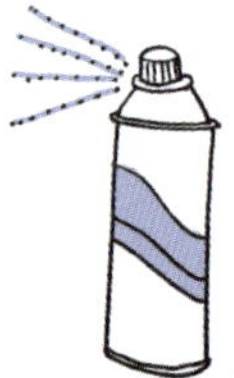

spray

sprain

split

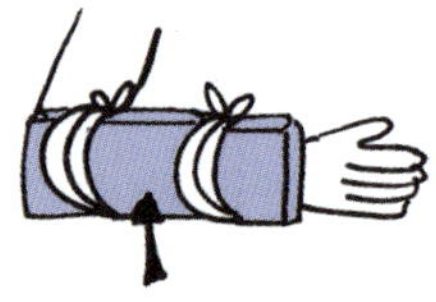

splint

In **spr****ing**, seeds **spr****out** and flowers bloom.

봄에는 씨앗이 싹을 틔우고 꽃이 피어난다.

They put a **spl****int** on my **sprain**ed wrist.

그들은 내 삔 발목에 부목을 대었다.

I'd like to have a banana **spl****it** with some whipped cream **spray**ed on top!

생크림을 올린 바나나 스플릿 먹을래요!

130

squ&shr

square / **squ**id / **squ**eeze /
squeak / **squ**irt
shrimp / **shr**ink / **shr**ed

square

squid

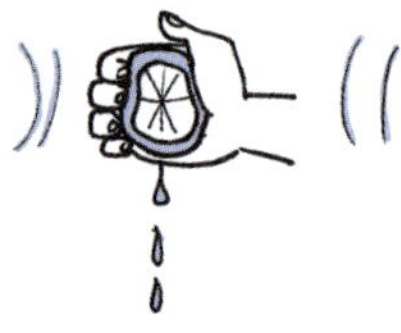

squeeze

squeak

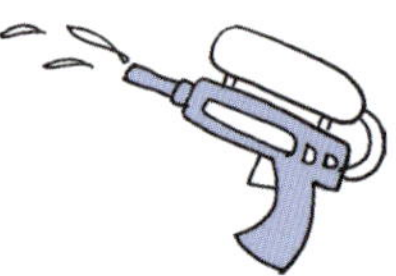

squirt

shrimp

shrink

shred

The **squid squirt**ed ink at the **shrimp**.

그 오징어는 새우를 향해 먹물을 내뿜었다.

When I **squeeze**d it, it **squeak**ed and **shrank** down.

내가 그것을 쥐어짜자 그것은 찍 소리를 내며 작아졌다.

Shred the **square**-shaped ham, please.

네모 모양 햄을 채 썰어 주세요.

soft C

**face / race / slice / ice /
nice / place / dance**

face

race

slice

ice

nice

place

dance

Would you like a **slice** of **ice** cream cake?

아이스크림 케이크 한 조각 먹을래?

His **face** turned red after the **race** across the town.

마을 횡단 경주 후에 그의 얼굴은 벌겋게 달아올랐다.

There's a **nice place** where you can drink, **dance**, and make friends.

술 마시고 춤도 추고 친구도 사귈 수 있는 좋은 곳이 있어.

132

soft g

ag**e** / **c**a**g**e** / **p**a**g**e** / **w**a**g**e** /
sta**g**e** / **g**ene

age

cage

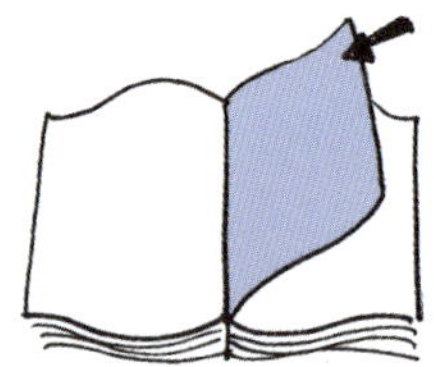

page

wage

stage

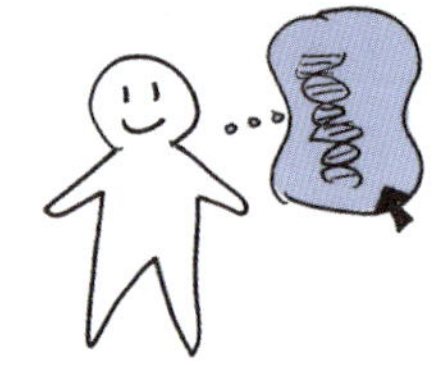

gene

Given their **age**, their **wage**s must be pretty low.

그들의 나이를 생각하면 임금이 꽤 낮을 거야.

Go to **page** 10 and read about how **gene**s work.

10쪽을 펼쳐서 유전자가 어떻게 기능하는지 읽어 보세요.

I'd rather be locked in a **cage** than dance on that **stage**.

나는 그 무대에서 춤 추느니 우리에 갇혀있는 쪽을 택하겠어.

133

tion & sion

fiction / **sec**tion /
invention / **men**tion
decision / **man**sion

fic**tion**

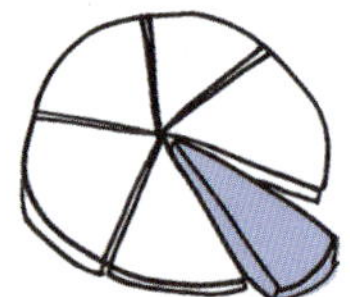

sec**tion**

inven**tion**

men**tion**

deci**sion**

man**sion**

He did **mention** something about the **invention**.

그가 그 발명에 대해 확실히 뭔가 말하기는 했어.

You can find that book in the **fiction section** over there.

저쪽에 있는 소설 구역에서 그 책을 찾으실 수 있습니다.

They made a **decision** to buy a large **mansion** for the people in need.

그들은 어려운 사람들을 위해 대저택을 사기로 결정했다.

134

ture & sure

picture / **mix**ture / **tex**ture / **sculp**ture / **cul**ture **trea**sure / **plea**sure

pic**ture**

mix**ture**

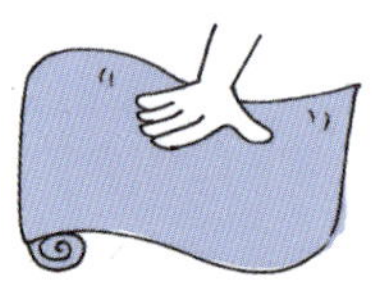

tex**ture**

sculp**ture**

cul**ture**

trea**sure**

plea**sure**

The **tex**ture of the **mix**ture was soft and smooth.

그 혼합물의 질감은 부드럽고 매끄러웠다.

Her **pic**tures and **sculp**tures show what's unique about her **cul**ture.

그녀의 그림과 조각품은 그녀가 속한 문화의 특이한 점을 보여준다.

It gave him great **plea**sure to find the box of **trea**sure in his backyard.

뒷마당에서 보물상자를 찾아낸 것은 그에게 큰 기쁨을 가져다주었다.

135

dge

edge / **fu**dge / **do**dge /
fridge / **nu**dge / **lo**dge

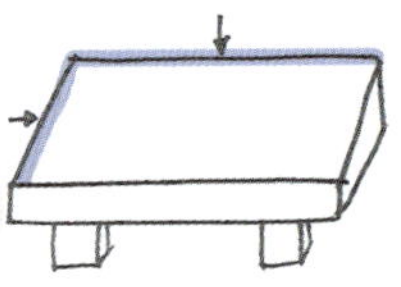

e**dge**

fu**dge**

do**dge**

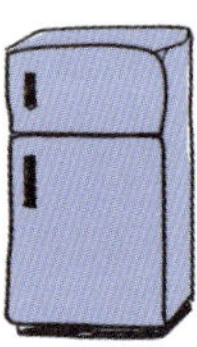

fri**dge**

nu**dge**

lo**dge**

Have some cool **fudge**. It's in the **fridge**.

차가운 퍼지 좀 먹어. 냉장고에 있어.

I **nudge**d him, but he **dodge**d behind me.

나는 팔꿈치로 그를 찔렀지만, 그는 내 뒤로 재빨리 피했다.

The old **lodge** was built on the **edge** of the cliff.

그 낡은 오두막은 벼랑 끝에 지어졌다.

INDEX (A~Z)

Sight Words

C

scab	41	ship	56	skirt	121
scalp	73	shirt	121	skull	41
scan	41	shock	56	skunk	77
scared	127	shocked	83	sky	117
scoff	41	shop	56	slam	47
scold	97	short	123	sled	47
scowl	112	shot	56	sleepy	118
scratch	128	shout	111	sleigh	88
scream	128	show	96	slice	131
scrub	128	shred	130	slid	47
sculpture	134	shrimp	130	slim	47
scum	41	shrink	130	slip	47
sea	100	shut	56	slit	47
section	133	sick	14	slot	47
selfie	102	sift	70	sloth	65
sell	25	sigh	91	slow	96
send	75	sight	91	slug	47
set	22	silk	72	smack	37
share	127	sing	66	small	115
shark	119	singing	67	smell	37
sharp	119	sip	11	smelly	78
she	98	sipped	83	smock	37
sheep	99	sit	10	smog	37
shell	56	skate	84	smoke	93
shin	56	skim	41	smug	37

A

a, about, across, after, against, ago, all, almost, along, already, also, always, an, and, another, any, anyone, are, around, as, at, away

B

back, be, became, been, before, begun, behind, beside, better, bit, both, brother, building, built, but, buy, by

C

came, can, can't, Christmas, come, coming, cool, could, couldn't

D

day, decides, did, didn't, do, does, doesn't, don't, down, during

E

each, enough, even, every, everything

F

family, father, find, fine, for, found, friend, friends, from, full

G

gave, get, gets, give, given, gives, go, goes, going, gone, good, got, guess

H

had, has, have, he, he'd, he's, heard, heavy, help, helped, her, here, hi, him, his, house, how

I

I, I'd, I'll, I'm, if, in, into, is, isn't, it, it's

J

just

K

kept, known

L

large, leave, less, let, let's, like, likes, little, long, look, looking, looks, lot, love

M

made, make, makes, many, may, me, might, mind, mine, mom, more, move, Mrs., much, must, my

N

near, need, never, new, news, no, not, now

O

of, off, often, oh, OK, on, once, one, ones, only, onto, open, or, other, our, out, over

P

people, plays, please, possibly, pretty, put

Q

quite

R

rather, really

S

said, same, saw, say, see, seems, seen, seriously, she, she's, should, since, so, some, something, sometimes, somewhat, son, sound, still, stuck

T

take, than, that, that's, the, their, them, themselves, then, there, there's, these, they, they've, thing, things, this, those, though, through, time, to, together, too, took, town

U

under, unique, until, up, upon, us, use

V

very

W

want, wants, was, wasn't, watched, water, way, we, we'll, we're, we've, well, well, went, were, what, what's, when, where, which, while, who, who'd, why, will, wind, with, woman, won't, word, work, would, wouldn't, wrong

Y

years, yes, yet, you, you'd, you'll, you're, your, yours, yourself